HE RESTORES MY SOUL

A Forty-Day Journey Toward Personal Renewal

Jennifer Kennedy Dean

B&H Publishing Group
Nashville TN

978-0-8054-2027-2

Published by B&H Publishing Group, Nashville, Tennessee
Editorial Team: Vicki Crumpton, Janis Whipple, Kim Overcash
Typesetting: Desktop Miracles, Dallas, Texas

Published in association with the literary agency of Alive Communications, Inc.,
1465 Kelly Johnson Blvd., Suite 320, Colorado Springs, CO 80902

Dewey Decimal Classification: 269
Subject Heading: MEDITATIONS / PERSONAL RETREATS
Library of Congress Card Catalog Number: 99-20298

Unless otherwise indicated, all Scripture references are from The Holy Bible, New International Version (NIV), copyright © 1973, 1978, 1984 by International Bible Society. Other versions cited include the NASB, the New American Standard Bible, © the Lockman Foundation, 1960, 1962, 1963, 1968, 1971, 1972, 1973, 1975, 1978, used by permission; and the King James Bible.

Library of Congress Cataloging-in-Publication Data

Dean, Jennifer Kennedy.
    He restores my soul : a forty-day journey toward personal renewal / Jennifer Kennedy Dean
        p. cm.
    ISBN 0-8054-2027-4 (pbk.)
    1. Meditations. 2. Retreats. I. Title
    BV4832.2.D396   1999
    269'.6—dc21

                                                            99-20298
                                                            CIP

15 16 17 18 19 20   11 10 09 08 07

Table of Contents

Dedication

To my sons: Brantley, Kennedy, and Stinson.

You bring such joy to my life and I delight
in seeing you becoming men after God's own heart.

Acknowledgments

I'd like to thank those whose faithful intercession
and encouragement fuel my journey:

My parents, Don and Audrey Kennedy—always there.

My prayer partner, Mary Medley—fellow adventurer in faith.

My Tuesday night prayer group—my prayer lab.

My friends, Jeanne and Dale Parrott—spiritual cheerleaders.

My personal intercessor, Janelle Lapaglia—faithful, steadfast, true.

My husband, Wayne—friend and partner.

My ministry partner, Lyn Olson—doer of the Word.

My church, First Baptist Church of Blue Springs, MO—wonderful,
open-hearted gift from God.

Your holy Fire now burns within
And purges every secret sin;
My life the bush, Your Life the Flame
That leaves me nevermore the same.

A heart like Yours, my one desire;
Do Your work, Refiner's Fire.

—Jennifer Kennedy Dean

Using This Book

In this book, those seeking a fresh perspective on personal, contemplative prayer will find eternal and time-tested truths cast in new forms.

Perhaps you're struggling with the discipline of a daily time with the Lord. This book will help jump-start your devotional life by giving you new ways to approach your daily prayer time. Perhaps your daily time with the Lord is consistent. This book will give you a new way of looking at listening prayer that can energize and revitalize your personal devotional life.

In section 1 you will:

- Discover the concept of "retreating" on a daily basis.
- Learn to take your retreat into your day.
- Learn to find the inner sanctuary of your soul that is always accessible.
- Learn the elements of retreating: centering, ceremony, and celebration.
- Learn the scriptural significance of the number forty.

In section 2, you will make a forty-day commitment to daily retreating with the Lord. You will spend those forty days learning to respond to the Father's now-speaking voice calling you to discern the secret to spiritual renewal and to experience the power of the resurrection.

In section 3, you will find a detailed plan for a time of personal retreat during which you will commit an extended block of time—twenty-four hours if possible—to focusing on the Father's voice.

Preface

I was going through a difficult time in my life. One problem followed another. Pain piled upon pain. Relief, it seemed, was nowhere in sight. One morning, as I poured out my heart—my hurt, my confusion, my doubts—to the Father, it seemed to me that He asked, "Jennifer, what is it that you want?" The answer seemed obvious to me. I wanted relief. I wanted God to fix things. I wanted my circumstances to line up with my expectations.

When I had finished explaining to God just exactly what I wanted Him to do, His quiet inner voice said, "Is that all? Those are such little things. Won't you let Me give you more than that? What else do you want? Look deeper. Look underneath all of your demands and expectations. What more do you want?"

I took an inward journey. I asked the Holy Spirit to lead me into all truth. I examined each need or want in my life by asking myself, "Why do I need or want this? What do I expect this to bring to my life?" I developed this "formula," for lack of a better word: If I had (request), then I would be

_____.

I found that I had filled in my blanks with words like "secure," "happy," "carefree," "valued," "at peace," and "confident." Then I recognized that everything I longed for was waiting for me in Him. I had been asking God to meet the needs in my life with something other than Himself. For the first time I began to truly understand that God is all. I learned this important truth: I cannot know the desire of my heart until I know the heart of my desire. The heart of every desire is a longing for God. As this revelation grew in me, the Spirit whispered to me again, "What is it that you want?" This time I cried out, "Father, I want You."

Then came His answer. "I've always known what you wanted. I've always been intent on giving you what you truly want. Everything in your life, good and bad, is there so that I can give you Myself. Even before you recognized it, that was your heart's cry."

At that time my desire for the fullness of God became so intense that I was willing to walk any road or pay any price to find it. I became willing, even eager, to let go of everything else I had valued to possess the kingdom. The Spirit formed within me this heart's cry:

A heart like Yours, my one desire;
Do Your work, Refiner's Fire.

From this ever-increasing desire of my heart, I write this book. I pray that, even in the inadequacy and ineptness of my words, you will discover the liberating truth that everything you long for and everything you need is already yours in Him. I have asked the Spirit to take my meager word-offering and multiply its impact in your life by His amazing power. I have asked Him to use His Word to restore your soul.

SECTION 1
BEGINNINGS

*Spoken prayer will not reach its potential
unless it is grounded in listening prayer.
In listening prayer, spoken prayer is born.*

Invitation

Blessed are those . . . who have set
their hearts on pilgrimage. (Psalm 84:5)

I invite you to join me on a journey of the soul, to set your soul on pilgrimage and watch the continuous unfolding of the power and provision of God. Watch Him put adventure into your moments. Discover the bold, audacious, dynamic life of Christ in you, waiting to be released through you. Choose the way of faith.

Jesus is the author, pioneer, and leader of our faith. "Let us fix our eyes on Jesus, the author and perfecter of our faith" (Heb. 12:2). Scripture, in Hebrews 2:10 and 12:2, uses a compound word: *arche* (beginning) and *ago* (to lead). It means "one who blazes a trail, a pioneer, and a leader." You and I are not blazing the trail. We are under the protection and guidance of Him who has blazed the trail and now has returned to lead us along it.

My brethren! Do you understand what it means that the Father . . . has made Jesus the leader of our salvation. *Jesus is responsible for you.* Take Him and trust Him as your leader. *The great need in one who follows a leader is a tender, teachable spirit.* Rejoice that you have such a leader . . . that He might lead you in the blessed path that brought Him, and will bring you as surely, to the glory of the Father.

And remember who this leader is—the Son of God, the divine maker and upholder of all things. Not only the Son of Man, as a leader outside of us, influencing us by example and instruction, by authority and kindness does He guide us. No, but as the Son of God who works in us by His Spirit, yea who Himself dwells within us. Even as it was God who worked in Him and perfected Him, will He, as God, now work in us and perfect us.[1] (italics added)

Do you see? This soul pilgrimage is not wandering, but a directed venture along an identifiable path. "Who, then, is the man that fears the LORD? / He will instruct him in the way chosen for him" (Ps. 25:12). As you journey, you are walking a path chosen just for you. Your journey has been charted in advance, the trail has been blazed, and the path is engraved in your heart. Your path—the path set out for you—was born into you when you were born into the kingdom of God. It is encoded in your spiritual DNA. All you need to do is yield yourself to your Pioneer-leader. The way is not a document; the way is Jesus Himself, who dwells in you and operates in you by His present-tense power. When you walk in Him, you have found your way—the way chosen for you. Bring nothing with you except a tender, teachable spirit. Jesus, your trail-blazing guide, is responsible for you.

The purpose of the journey is to learn how to open more of your life to God's power; to become progressively more accessible and receptive to Him. In the course of your travel, you will discover that—day-by-day, little-by-little—your soul is being restored. You will find yourself putting aside the old behavior patterns and worn-out thoughts and embracing the ever-fresh life within you. You will find His promise becoming your reality: "He restores my soul. / He guides me in paths of righteousness / for his name's sake" (Ps. 23:3).

Specifically I invite you to use this book as a resource for a forty-day retreating experience. Learn the art of retreating. Follow Jesus as your leader, who, in His days on earth, retreated daily and periodically retreated for extended times. He blazed the trail. Follow Him as, from within you by His Spirit, He calls you to retreat with Him regularly and to experience the same refreshing, the same renewal, the same soul-restoring power that He experienced in retreat.

The Art of Retreating

What is a retreat?

To retreat means to intentionally withdraw for a time from the pace of day-to-day living with the aim of listening to God's now-speaking voice. Retreat can become a part of your daily experience, not just an occasional getaway. For the believer who is seeking the fullness of life in Christ, this intentional and planned solitude and silence must be daily.

> There is power in silence, the very power of God. . . . It is in the silence that the Holy Spirit does his most powerful work, making permanent what otherwise would have been evanescent; impressing truths as a potter makes an impress on clay; registering on mind and conscience what has just been said in words.[2]

Anne Morrow Lindbergh, in *Gift from the Sea,* made this observation: "Even those whose lives had appeared to be ticking unperturbably under their smiling clock-faces were often trying, like me, to evolve another rhythm with more creative pauses in it, more adjustment to their individual needs, and new and more alive relationships to themselves as well as others."[3] I would change some of Lindbergh's wording to more accurately express what retreating with the Father produces. We begin to evolve a new rhythm with more listening, and thus creative pauses in it. Our relationships are new and more alive because we are abiding in love Himself and His love is the wellspring of ours. We find ourselves spontaneously living a more Christ-referenced life. Daily retreating feeds and strengthens the undercurrent of prayer that is always flowing through those in whom Christ dwells.

In retreating, we focus on listening prayer. Learning how to be open to God's present voice is the key ingredient in powerful praying and powerful living. Let Him shape your thoughts and form your desires as you surrender your heart to be clay in His hands. Let Him restore your soul with the power of His now-speaking voice. Just as His voice brought order out of chaos and light out of darkness and form out of formlessness, it will bring the completeness for which you are longing. Only when we understand the power of His voice will we learn the purpose of listening prayer. We make a mistake when we think that the *primary* purpose of prayer is for us to say things to God. Rather, it is for God to say things to us. His promise is this:

"'I will answer you and tell you great and unsearchable things you do not know'" (Jer. 33:3).

Father, push back the noise. Your secrets come wrapped in silence.[4]

What are the elements of a retreat?
A retreat is a time of solitude and silence and it contains within it three elements: centering, ceremony, and celebration. Examine these more closely with me.

Centering
Centering is prayer that takes time to turn inward to the indwelling presence of God. In centering prayer one nurtures the awareness that the Holy of Holies, the dwelling place of the Most High, is within each believer. Each believer has become the temple of Jehovah, the place where His name dwells. In centering prayer we remember that He is not a God far away, but that His very name is Immanuel, which means "God with us."

> Don't you know that you yourselves are God's temple and that God's Spirit lives in you? (1 Cor. 3:16)

Centering prayer is recognizing and embracing His nearness. In centering prayer we learn to say, "But as for me, the nearness of God is my good" (Ps. 73:28, NASB). As we let the truth of His living presence seep into the pores of our consciousness so that it becomes solid reality for us, we find Him hovering and brooding over our intellects and bringing forth new levels of understanding and insight. John Woolman wrote in his journal about this experience: "As I lived under the cross and simply followed the openings of truth, my mind from day to day was more enlightened. . . . While I silently ponder on that change which I found in me, I find no language equal to it, nor any means to convey to another a clear idea of it. . . . And as I was thus humbled and disciplined under the cross my understanding became more strengthened to know the language of the pure Spirit which moves upon the intellectual deep."[5]

Centering prayer is not centering on myself but on the Lord who dwells in me and longs to impart His life in all its fullness to me at every level of my being: spiritual, emotional, intellectual, and relational. Centering prayer is turning my eyes upon Jesus to look full in His wonderful face[6] and realizing that His wonderful face is not far away, but is in my very own heart.

Ceremony

There is a ritual element in retreating, but it is not empty ritual. Holy rituals, outward forms that express true inward worship, play an important role in the retreat event. Ceremony helps us focus and transition from one mode to another, from being engaged outwardly to being engaged inwardly. Your retreat rituals, or ceremonies, will be simple but meaningful to you. Each retreatant will develop his or her own ceremonies and will understand their purpose—to help express the inexpressible and to detach from the pull of life's demands.

Some ceremonies will be outward. For example, once you decide on a place and time for your daily retreat, going to that place at that time will be a ceremony that will quickly move you into your listening posture. That place will probably be a place in your home, but at your retreat time it becomes sacred. Part of your ceremony might be sipping a cup of your favorite tea or lighting the fire in your fireplace. I like to use scented candles—not for any religious reason, but because I enjoy the fragrance and I like the ambience. I retreat early in the morning, so part of my ceremony begins before I go to bed at night. I clear out my retreat space and make sure it's inviting. I put out my favorite old quilt to wrap up in when I get there. I program my coffee pot to have my coffee ready when I get up. I make sure my Bible and prayer journal are there. Even setting my alarm for my retreat hour is part of the ceremony. All of this puts me in the frame of mind that, without question, I will be up and retreating in the morning.

Journaling and Bible reading are ceremonies that give texture to retreating. It will be important for you to journal your thoughts, observations, insights, questions, and prayers. In fact, the words *journal* and *journey* come from the same root that has the sense of "day-by-day" or "a day at a time." Your journal records your journey. Find your own way of journaling. Your journal entries may vary from day to day. Some of my journal entries are nothing more than sentence fragments. Some are questions. Others are what I need to say to God, and still others are what He is saying to me. Sometimes I'm recording occurrences, other times I'm recording doubts. Sometimes I even draw pictures (although not with much skill). Most often, I am writing down thoughts and insights from the Word.

Another ceremony might be the use of other resources you bring to retreat. You may bring a devotional book like this one. You might sing worshipful hymns or choruses or listen to a recording of worshipful music. Develop your own external ceremonies.

Part of your ceremony will be internal. You will learn how to enter the "amazing inner sanctuary of the soul," as Thomas R. Kelley referred to it.[7] God has created you with a mind that is able to picture truth. He has filled the Scriptures with visual words and detailed descriptions. Let your mind picture the truth of His presence. See yourself bowing before Him or talking face-to-face with Jesus, like you would talk to your friend.

Don't be frightened away from this visual kind of praying by New Age and other eastern religions' use of visualization. It is nothing like what I am describing. You are not trying to create a reality by visualizing it. You are experiencing a spiritual reality in a way that God intended for you to enter into it, by using the brain He created with the wonderful and awesome capacity to think visually. Your picturing of this reality, described in the Word of God, neither helps God nor creates power. It only allows you to enter into the fact of His presence. Do not allow a twisting of this truth by some to deny you the practice of visual prayer.

Discover and create your own internal ceremonies. For example, you might:

- Read about an occurrence from the life of Christ from one of the Gospels. Imagine yourself as one of the characters in the story and let your mind walk through the details of the event, seeing it as if you were there—as if the event were unfolding in front of your eyes. What new insights do you gain?

- Mentally list the scheduled events in the upcoming day. Deliberately surrender each to God, asking Him to do His will in His way.
- Name specific things about which you are anxious. As you name each one, let the naming of it be your act of laying it at His feet.
- Take the time to remember a moment of joy, humor, or fun. Relive it in detail and experience the Father's delight in your pleasure. Thank Him.

Celebration

The word *celebrate* is from a Latin word, *celebrare*, which means "to frequent." Celebration implies coming back to the same place over and over again. It means to repeat an action. We have added to it the sense of rejoicing. In retreating, we are learning to frequent the presence of the Father. We are learning to find our joy and highest good at His feet. His voice will awaken joy in us and we will find ourselves celebrants of His nearness. We learn to embrace His invitation: "'Arise, come, my darling; / my beautiful one, come with me'" (Song of Sol. 2:13).

Retreating can be boiled down to this simple definition: Celebrating the Most High.

What time of day is best for retreating?

Early morning is the optimum time for retreating. There may be health or scheduling issues that make early morning impossible. If so, don't feel guilty. Early morning, last thing before bed, during your lunch break—any time that you deliberately set aside as retreat time will be effective. However, if at all possible, consider making early morning your time for retreat. Early morning lends itself to silence and solitude more easily than any other part of the day. Silence and solitude are the foundations of retreat. In the early morning you are less likely to be harried or distracted by other needs. The act of getting out of bed for no other reason but to spend time listening to the Spirit is, in itself, worship. It is a statement of priority. William Law set forth the standard in *A Serious Call to a Devout and Holy Life:*

I take it for granted that every Christian that is in health is up early in the morning, for it is much more reasonable to suppose a person is up early because he is a Christian than because he is a labourer, or a servant, or has business that wants him. . . . For if he is to be blamed as a slothful drone that rather chooses the lazy indulgences of sleep than to perform his proper share of worldly business, how much is he to be reproached that had rather lie folded up in a bed than be raising up his heart to God in acts of praise and adoration?[8]

To fully enter into the experience of retreating will require discipline. It will require that you commit to the actions of retreating. Do not let laziness rob you of the life that can be yours if you spend time listening to the Spirit.

The time you set aside for retreating is sacred. Whether it is early morning or not, the block of time you have scheduled for retreat should be inviolate. If you had a very important appointment with the doctor, with your boss, or with someone else, you would think it rude not to hold to it no matter what else came along. So it should be with your retreat time. Make the appointment and don't break it.

How long should a daily retreat be?

You are on the path chosen for you. Your journey is not someone else's journey. There are no rule books or rigid structures to define personal retreats. Start with a time frame that feels acceptable to you. If, like I am, you are an introvert, you will wish for hours of daily retreat. If you are an extrovert, you may have to force yourself to consider any amount of time given to solitude and silence. What amount of time feels right to you? Maybe fifteen minutes or thirty minutes. Maybe an hour.

My guess, based on the experiences of numerous people, is that even if you start out with only a few minutes of retreat, you will soon find that an hour of retreat has passed too quickly. Once you begin to learn the power of the "living voice," time in His presence will fly. The next step will be to learn how to take your retreat with you into the day. Retreating, you will learn, is not withdrawing from life, but instead is finding the ability to plunge into life fearlessly and fully equipped.

How can I use body posture to express worship during my retreat?
One of the benefits of private, personal retreat time is that you can be completely uninhibited in your worship style. Because you are alone, you won't have to consider whether your expressions of worship will be distracting to someone else or worry about what someone else might think of them. You may find that you feel free to worship in ways that will help you express your openness to God's power in deeper ways.

In many ways, we use our bodies to communicate emotions. A person's body language can often communicate at a deeper level than conversation alone allows. The Scriptures describe numerous postures of worship. Perhaps you will find it refreshing to physically assume some of these worship postures; or perhaps you will find it more conducive to prayer if you imagine yourself in a worship posture. Letting your body express worship is another type of ceremony that may enhance your retreat time.

Consider some of these scriptural worship postures:

- Kneel in His presence
    Come, let us bow down in worship,
        let us kneel before the LORD our Maker. (Ps. 95:6)

- Spread out your hands toward heaven
    I spread out my hands to you;
        my soul thirsts for you like a parched land. (Ps. 143:6)

- Lift up your hands
    Lift up your hands in the sanctuary
        and praise the LORD. (Ps. 134:2)

- Stand before Him
    Who may ascend the hill of the LORD?
        Who may stand in his holy place? (Ps. 24:3)

- Fall on your face before Him
    When I saw him, I fell at his feet as though dead. (Rev. 1:17)

What tools do I need for my retreat?

Again, you will design your own retreats according to what is appealing to you and conducive to worship for you. Essentials are your Bible, a prayer journal, and a writing utensil. Other tools might be:

- devotional book
- sketch pad and pencils
- worshipful music and something to play it on (but don't fill your whole retreat with sound)
- recordings of nature sounds
- candles
- a hymn or chorus book

How do I take retreating into my day?

Once daily retreating becomes your habit, you will find that you can engage in mini-retreats. These mini-retreats will call you back to the Father throughout the day. A retreat might be as simple as letting the thought, "You are my one desire" take root. You might be able to pull away from others for several minutes, close your eyes, and engage in centering prayer.

Carry a conveniently sized journal and Bible with you. You can learn to retreat in airports, in waiting rooms, at your desk, in your car—anywhere. You can make quick excursions into the inner sanctuary for restoration and refreshment.

These mini-retreats will be effective if they are the outgrowth of extended daily times of retreating.

> While many private prayers, in the nature of things, must be short; while public prayers, as a rule ought to be short and condensed; while there is ample room for and value put on ejaculatory prayer—yet in our private communions with God *time is a*

feature essential to its value. Much time spent with God is the secret of all successful praying. Prayer which is felt as a mighty force is the mediate or immediate product of much time spent with God. Our short prayers owe their point and efficiency to the long ones that have preceded them. The short prevailing prayer cannot be prayed by one who has not prevailed with God in a mightier struggle of long continuance.[9] (italics added)

What E. M. Bounds says about prayer—that time is a feature essential to its value—is true of retreating, which is really listening prayer. Retreating can become a powerful tool and can be used periodically throughout the day when it has been fostered by much time spent with God.

Your retreating experiences will color your whole life. They will be effective not only when you are in retreat but also in gradually and steadily changing your entire approach to living. As your soul is being restored to wholeness, that wholeness will be manifested in your daily life. You will discover what Evan Drake Howard called "centering faith." He defined its role: "This centering faith not only overcomes despair—it also creates joy and sends ordinary people into the world as agents of hope and peace."[10]

At some deep level, you will always be retreating with Him. That sense of His presence, the experience of His nearness, and oneness in purpose with Him cease to be occasional and conscious and become the backdrop against which all of life is played out. Thomas R. Kelley described this process as "unworded but habitual orientation of all one's self about Him who is the focus."[11]

What about talking to God?

Listening to God is the primary element in retreating. But what about talking to God? Is that also part of the retreating experience? Yes, of course. Talking to God is important; however, it's easy to overemphasize what we say to God and underplay what He says to us. The primary element is His voice. What I say in prayer is shaped by what He says to me, by the thoughts He awakens in me, by the concerns He implants in my heart, and by the insights He births. His life flows through me and produces prayer. I pray in response to Him.

Typically our humanity is so eager to express our opinions or plead for the answers to our needs that we rush through worship and listening and waiting so that we can get to the important part—what we want to say.

Keep in mind two things when you weigh your words to God in the prayer equation. First, your retreating times will not be the only opportunity for you to talk to God. Everything that comes into your day, every thought that crosses your mind can be directed to God and become prayer. To pray effectively and powerfully, you don't have to give God a long list of everything that needs to be done in each situation. You just have to turn it toward Him. Simply saying the name of Jesus will often be the only prayer word you need. That one word speaks volumes and releases all the power of heaven.

Second, you do not need to articulate your needs and desires for God to know them. If you don't have the opportunity to list your requests, they do not go unnoticed by God. "All my longings lie open before you, O Lord; / my sighing is not hidden from you" (Ps. 38:9). God *does* tell you to articulate your requests so that, in the process of describing your needs or desires, He can clarify them for you. Sometimes your listening prayer will be the Father asking, "What do you want? Tell Me about your burden; tell Me about your need; tell Me about your desire." As you put your thoughts into words and sentences, you gain a new vantage point. As His voice joins with yours and His wisdom flows through your intellect, truth becomes clear. In *Letters to Malcolm,* C. S. Lewis quotes these anonymous lines:

> I seek in myself the things I hoped to say,
> But, lo! my wells are dry.
>
> Then, seeing me empty, you forsake
> The listener's role and through
> My dumb lips breathe and into utterance wake
> The thoughts I never knew.[12]

When prayer evolves to the place where it is no longer *me* separate from *God*—two distinct parties bridging a chasm with words, then a settled peace takes hold and continually guards heart and mind. I am not saying that you become God or become a god or become your own god! In one sense, you and God will always be separate because only God is God. But He wants your life to become so abandoned to Him that your life becomes a vessel for His life. He wants you to learn a surrender so complete that He can think His thoughts in you, He can express His yearnings through yours, and He can speak through your words.

> There come times when prayer pours forth in volumes and orig-
> inality such as we cannot create. It rolls through us like a mighty
> tide. Our prayers are mingled with a vaster word, a Word that at
> one time was made flesh. We pray, and yet it is not we who pray,
> but a Greater who prays in us. . . . All we can say is, Prayer is tak-
> ing place, and I am given to be in the orbit.[13]

There are certainly times for worded prayer, times of prayer when the articulating of it is critical. I have written previously about that kind of prayer. However, this book addresses contemplative, listening prayer. I am convinced of this: Spoken prayer will not reach its potential unless it is grounded in listening prayer. In listening prayer, spoken prayer is born.

Using the *He Restores My Soul* Forty-Day Retreat Plan

In the following pages, you will find forty daily meditations, reflection questions, and journaling exercises. I challenge you to commit to forty days of daily retreating, ending with an optional extended retreat, which section 3 details. Make this commitment alone, or ask others to make the commitment with you.

The devotional material is divided into seven-day segments, with five days of readings per week. Every sixth day of each segment will be reflective exercises and review questions. Every seventh day will be a day for you to meet as a group or with your partner to discuss the week, or if you are soloing on this journey, the seventh day will be a reflective day for you to solidify what your week has brought into focus. This seven-day format aims to fit easily into your weekly routine and habits.

Why forty days?

The number *forty* has strong symbolism in the Scriptures. Forty is a number associated with cleansing, purifying, and preparation. For example, at the time of the flood, the rain came down for forty days. Moses spent forty years in the desert between his exile from Egypt and his call to lead Israel. The Israelites spent forty years in the desert between Egypt and Canaan. Jesus spent forty days in the desert before entering His public ministry. In each of these instances, the time was a significant transition from one period of life to another:

- The earth, after forty days and nights, was cleansed and able to start afresh.
- Moses left Egypt a murderer, having trusted in his own skill and ability to save, and returned forty years later, humbled and trusting only in God's power to save.
- God took Israel out of Egypt, but it took forty years for God to take Egypt out of Israel.
- Jesus spent forty days retreating with the Father as He transitioned from private life to public ministry.

Will you make this commitment to forty days of opening your life fully to the Father? Will you consecrate forty days and declare them sacred? Will you make the commitment to retreat with the Father every day for forty days?

In making this commitment, don't fall into the trap of legalism. If you miss a day, don't decide that you've failed. Pick up where you left off and move forward. Let these forty days be days of celebrating the presence of Christ, not days of drudgery and duty.

A daily plan

1. Write down the beginning and ending days of your forty-day commitment. Log them in your journal and/or on your calendar.

2. Decide what time of day you will set aside for your daily retreat. Also decide how much time you will commit each day to your retreat. Write these in your journal.

3. Think through how your retreat time will be structured. This structure will serve as a starting place. Each day, your retreat time may flow differently. Thinking through a basic structure ensures you will not waste your valuable retreat time deciding what to do. I propose the following structure as a springboard:

   A. Centering: Start with centering prayer. Picture the presence of Jesus with you and let the reality of Him take hold of your heart and mind. Ask Him to guide you into all truth (John 16:13), to open your spiritual ears so that you can hear Him (Isa. 50:4), and to pour His thoughts out to you (Prov. 1:23).

   B. Meditation: Use the daily meditations as one of your retreat ceremonies and respond to the reflection questions.

   C. Celebration: Spend time worshiping in the inner sanctuary of your soul. Respond to the thoughts and emotions the Spirit stirs within you.

4. Add your own ceremonies and let your retreating time express your personality and own ways of celebrating. Enjoy being creative!

Meditations and terminology

The daily meditations will lead you through a journey that begins with brokenness and ends with fullness. In the course of these forty days you will explore certain scriptural terms. To ensure that these terms are commonly understood, let me define them.

Soul

The Greek word *psuche* is translated *soul*. In its New Testament use the soul refers to the mind, will, and emotions of a person; it is his or her human nature. It is the vehicle through which humans interact with one another as well as with the realm of ideas and emotions. It is the soul (mind, will, and emotions) of a person that produces his thought patterns, responses, decisions, and feelings. The soul, in itself, is not right or wrong. It is a necessary part of God's creation, meant to be the faculty through which God expresses Himself. God intended the human soul to be filled with and ruled by Him.

Spirit *(pneuma)* and soul *(psuche)* are different, and Scripture differentiates between them (see Heb. 4:12; 1 Thess. 5:23). Yet they are often used interchangeably. In the born-again believer, the spirit and soul are to function in tandem, fulfilling God's purpose and design for them. People are not "spirits" in isolation from a soul, but spiritual beings acting through their souls. Therefore, the words *spirit* and *soul* are often used in this context, meaning the two operating as one integrated whole (e.g., James 2:26; 1 Pet. 3:4; 2 Cor. 7:13).

Because of sin, the human soul, in its natural state, is opposed to God and unable to submit itself to His rule. Instead of expressing the life of God, the unredeemed human soul expresses the self-centered, self-worshiping, self-involved, self-focused, self-trusting life that is the fundamental principle of all sin. The soul's self-life sets itself against God. The self-life says, "I will be; I will do; I will decide," in direct opposition to God who says, "Yield to My life in you—I will be; yield to My power in you—I will do; yield to My wisdom in you—I will decide."

The soul that is disconnected from the God-life that it was meant to contain has a false sense of freedom. In reality, the sin principle that directs it is its master; it is in bondage. Until the soul recognizes its true state, that of slave, it is deceived into believing that it masters itself. How is the soul's bondage exposed? "The law was added so that the trespass might increase" (Rom. 5:20). The word *increase* really means "come to the front; be exposed or put on display." The law served two purposes: (1) to expose sin by setting up the standard for righteousness, and (2) to prove the sinner's powerlessness over sin. "For I have the desire to do what is good, but I cannot carry it out" (Rom. 7:18).

Once the soul encounters the truth, dies to its sin-master, and receives the indwelling life of Christ, it embarks on the journey for which God created it—being filled with His presence and power and glory.

At the very moment that a person believes and accepts the atoning death and resurrection of Christ as his or her own, Christ comes to dwell in that believer in His spirit-form. He comes to make His home in the believer's spirit (the aspect of humans through which they have consciousness of God and fellowship with Him) with the intent of progressively filling, saturating, permeating, and flooding the believer's soul with His life.

Eternal salvation is fully completed. However, salvation involves more than just ensuring eternal life. "Therefore he is able to save completely those who come to God through him, because he always lives to intercede for them" (Heb. 7:25). He saves *completely*—body, soul, and spirit. Salvation of the spirit is immediate, but salvation of the soul is progressive. The former sin-master of the soul has ingrained patterns of thought and behavior that must be eradicated. These flesh-patterns keep the believer from experiencing true, complete freedom.

Christ, from within, is in the process of saving you and me by His indwelling life (Rom. 5:10). He is restoring our souls to wholeness and freedom.

Flesh

The word *flesh* is used throughout the Old and New Testaments with a range of meanings, all of which refer to the aspects of humans that are not spirit-based. It refers, in the broadest sense, to our earthly nature that is expressed through our earthly bodies. *Flesh* sometimes means all human beings. Sometimes it means the earthly body. Most often it means the action of the human soul through the earthly body.

We can know the meaning of *flesh* from its context. For example, Scripture refers to Jesus "in the days of His flesh" (Heb. 5:7, NASB). This simply reminds us that Jesus operated through His human soul by the indwelling Spirit. No aspect of Jesus' soul was disconnected from the Father. The Scripture also tells us that God pours out His Spirit on "all flesh" (Acts 2:17, KJV), meaning that He pours out His Spirit on human beings; He puts His power into "jars of clay" (2 Cor. 4:7).

In these forty daily devotionals, I am using *flesh* to refer to the human soul when it is operating apart from divine influence. A person acting in the flesh will be thinking, feeling, reasoning, and responding apart from the indwelling life of Christ. That person's thoughts, actions, attitudes, and emotions will be generated from an earthly mindset instead of from a spiritual nature within.

The flesh, the points at which the soul is not filled with the divine life, must be crucified. It cannot be reformed. However, this crucifixion will lead to a resurrection. When the flesh-life in the soul has been crucified, the soul is free to live in resurrection power. Then the truth of Paul's radical statement in Galatians 2:20 becomes clear: "'I have been crucified with Christ and I no longer live, but Christ lives in me. The life I live in the body, I live by faith in the Son of God, who loved me and gave himself for me.'"

Crucifixion

The Word teaches that when a person is born into the kingdom of heaven, his or her sin nature enters into the crucifixion of Jesus. Paul said that "all of us who were baptized into Christ Jesus were baptized into his death" (Rom. 6:3). Paul clarified that Jesus' death was a death to sin as an active power (Rom. 6:10). I should count myself dead to sin as an active power, but alive to God in Christ Jesus (Rom. 6:11). This truth was accomplished once and for all at the cross. However, accessing the reality of that truth for daily living is an ongoing process.

Although I have been given a new nature, the life of Christ in me, some aspects of my soul still act according to flesh-patterns. The purpose of this ongoing salvation, then, is to root out the flesh and surrender it to crucifixion. Every time I am confronted with activity in my flesh, it is my choice either to allow it free reign or to hand it over to the Father to receive its death sentence.

How do I recognize flesh? When I become, for example, fearful, anxious, prideful, envious, divisive, territorial, or the like, I know that God has allowed my flesh to be brought out into the open so that I can choose to relinquish it for execution. In that moment, I decide either to turn my back on sin's power or to succumb to its pull. The external event or behavior that has engaged my flesh and put it on display is irrelevant. If a fleshly reaction can be elicited, then flesh is alive and well.

Crucifixion, by its very nature, is not a gentle death. Moments of crucifixion are painful. My flesh cries out for mercy. It is only because of the life of Christ "which so powerfully works in me" (Col. 1:29) and because He has taught me that *crucifixion is the prelude to resurrection* that I can ignore the pleas of my flesh.

Resurrection

Not only am I united with Christ in His death, but I am also united with Him in His resurrection.

> Or don't you know that all of us who were baptized into Christ Jesus were baptized into his death? We were therefore buried with him through baptism into death in order that, just as Christ was raised from the dead through the glory of the Father, we too may live a new life. If we have been united with him like this in his death, we will certainly also be united with him in his resurrection. (Rom. 6:3–5)

When I surrender to crucifixion (and sometimes I have to stay on the cross for a long time), the flesh in me dies, but the life of Christ then manifests His victorious power. The place of my weakness becomes the place of His greatest demonstration of power. Now my soul, instead of expressing the old, useless, self-serving Jennifer-life, is expressing Jesus-life.

Paul wrote, "For we know that our old self was crucified with him so that the body of sin might be done away with, that we should no longer be slaves to sin—because anyone who has died has been freed from sin" (Rom. 6:6–7). When my old self is crucified, "the body of sin" is "done away with." What does this mean? The "body of sin" means the body (the vehicle through which we perform) that belongs to sin; the body through which the old nature acts. When I enter into the crucifixion of Jesus, I do not receive a new earthly body. Externally I look just the same as I did before. But that old body has been made new internally. Now it no longer contains death; now it contains life.

Think of it like this: My computer is encased in an outer structure. When I look at my computer, I see its casing. That's how I recognize it as my computer. However, what really makes it *my* computer is its inner workings. If I were to take my computer to a technician and have him or her replace the old computer with an entirely new computer, but keep the outer structure, when I took the computer home, I would then have a brand new computer. It looks the same to my eyes, but it is a brand new creation. It has a new operating system; it runs new programs; it responds to different commands than before.

When Christ comes to be in my life, my body is no longer a body of sin. It is now a body of righteousness because the body of sin has been done away with. As I surrender more and more of my flesh to the cross, the new nature that dwells in me takes supremacy. "We always carry around in our body the death of Jesus, so that the life of Jesus may also be revealed in our body. For we who are alive are always being given over to death for Jesus' sake, so that his life may be revealed in our mortal body" (2 Cor. 4:10–11).

My soul acts through my body—my thoughts and my actions. As my soul is restored so that it is a container for the life of Christ, then my thoughts and actions reveal His life.

Heart

When Scripture uses the word *heart* in the spiritual sense, it refers to the inner person—the seat of thoughts and emotions. It makes sense to think of it as the mind—the instrument through which we process information and make decisions and imagine. In these forty days of devotionals, I am using the word *heart* to mean the command center of the soul.

SECTION 2
FORTY DAYS

The Spirit's quiet whisper
Bids me bow before Your throne
'Til my heart's deepest yearnings
Are the echo of Your own.
                    —Jennifer Kennedy Dean

WEEK 1

A Broken Heart

A broken and contrite heart,
O God, you will not despise. (Ps. 51:17)

Do you long to live in the Spirit's present-tense power?
Do you want to know the indwelling life of Christ as
your reality instead of an empty theology? Do you
want Jesus to fill you with Himself? Do you want the
living Lord to be someone you know, not just someone you believe in? Then embrace brokenness.

~ *Day 1* ~

Centering

Begin with centering prayer. Close your eyes and mentally move yourself into His presence. See Him with the eyes of your heart. Let this scriptural thought form the basis of your experience: "You have made known to me the path of life; / you will fill me with joy in your presence, / with eternal pleasures at your right hand" (Ps. 16:11).

Meditation

"Unless a kernel of wheat falls to the ground and dies,
it remains only a single seed.
But if it dies, it produces many seeds."
(John 12:24)

Brokenness is the ground from which spiritual power grows. Welcome brokenness. Embrace it. Don't fear it or resist it.

Only by breaking your outer layers—layers of pride, self-centeredness, and self-trust—can the inner power be released. The picture of a kernel of wheat falling into the ground to die is a perfect picture of brokenness. Where is the life in a seed? In the seed's embryo, which contains the blueprint for life. The husk, the tough outer layer in which the embryo is encased, must be broken down so that water and oxygen can reach the embryo, the life center. The outer layer must die so that the life contained within can emerge.

Your spirit-core, the part of you that is indwelt by God, is encased in a human nature, a nature prone to sin and with a bent toward unrighteousness. The Scriptures call your human nature, when it is acting in its own power, your flesh. The flesh must be broken so the Spirit of God in you can surface. Your old patterns of thinking and acting have to be broken so that the real power can emerge. Your old nature, your flesh, is a hindrance to you.

Paul called it a dead weight, like a dead body you have to drag around. "What a wretched man I am! Who will rescue me from this body of death?" (Rom. 7:24). Dead weight slows you down. God wants to free you from the dead weight of your flesh. Brokenness is the way to that freedom.

The psalmist expressed that God *loves* a broken heart, that He *desires* a broken heart. "A broken and contrite heart, / O God, you will not despise" (Ps. 51:17). The term *broken heart* does not mean sadness. It means a soul whose self-life has been exposed and its hold broken by the Spirit's power. Brokenness does not mean great sorrow. A person can be sorrowful without being broken. Brokenness does not mean humiliation. A person can be humiliated and not be broken. Brokenness does not mean discouragement. A person can be discouraged and still not be broken. Brokenness is an ongoing process. Daily the Spirit of God is revealing elements of the old nature still in operation. He is bringing out into the open fleshly ways of thinking and acting so He can break their hold over you, leaving you free to experience the victorious life of Christ in you.

True brokenness means losing all faith in your own abilities, abandoning all dependence on human resources, and disavowing all outward pretensions of righteousness to cling to the Spirit of God as if to a lifeline. The broken person—the person wholly dependent upon that indwelling life—will find that all of the resources of heaven and all of the Spirit's power are now at his disposal and, unless heaven's riches can be exhausted or the Spirit's power can be found wanting, he cannot come up short.

A broken person knows that God is the only worthwhile goal. A broken person stands before God as a living offering and declares, "You are my one desire."

- What does the phrase "spiritual power" mean to you? Define it in your own words.

  _____

  _____

  _____

• Where is spiritual power lacking in your life?

_____

_____

_____

• Are you willing to be broken so that you can know spiritual power? Describe your thoughts and feelings as you honestly face this question.

_____

_____

_____

Celebration

Write down one thought from your retreat time today about God's character or His work that awes you. What did He seem to highlight for you? Let that thought be the focus of your worship and celebration. Carry your celebration into your day.

_____

Centering

Begin with centering prayer. Close your eyes and mentally move yourself into His presence. See Him with the eyes of your heart. Let this scriptural thought form the basis of your experience: "Surely you have granted him eternal blessings / and made him glad with the joy of your presence" (Ps. 21:6).

Meditation

"Break up your unplowed ground." (Jer. 4:3)

- Read Matthew 13:3–9 and 18–23.

- In this parable, what kind of soil must the seed fall on in order to produce? (v. 8)

_____

_____

- How would you define "good soil"?

_____

_____

_____

Good soil is prepared soil. It is soil that has been plowed and is ready to receive the seed and give it a habitat in which it can flourish. Jesus compared His Word to a seed. A seed is just a seed and will remain nothing but a seed until it is placed in the proper environment. Once in the ground, the seed will metamorphose—become something altogether different. The proper environment for a seed is prepared ground. The proper environment for God's Word is a plowed heart.

"'Break up your unplowed ground,'" the Father says to you. Do you have a tendency to smooth over the topsoil of your heart instead of plowing it? Do you hide yourself from the Spirit's conviction by deflecting blame or rationalizing your actions? Scripture tells us that our hearts are experts at being devious. So much so that they fool us into believing our own justifications. God describes the unbroken heart, the heart filled with flesh-life, like this: "'The heart is deceitful above all things / and beyond cure. / Who can understand it?'" (Jer. 17:9). God wants to turn over the soil, to expose what's underneath, and to get it ready to receive.

God may be using circumstances in your life or people in your life to turn over the topsoil. You may feel as though the life you have worked so hard to keep smooth and presentable is being ripped up and destroyed. Maybe you've resisted the process. Maybe you keep trying to smooth it over and make it look like it used to, but to no avail. If you will surrender yourself to your heart's Plowman, you will see that you are being prepared to produce a harvest.

Is there a situation or a relationship in your life that you are continually managing, arranging, and manipulating, trying to force it into the mold of your expectations? Is there anything in your life about which you feel compelled to mislead people? If you have answered "yes" to either of these questions, then you will also answer "yes" to this: Are you worn-out? Drained? Anxious? Your soul was not created to run efficiently on flesh-power. Your flesh is working hard to resist the Spirit's breaking. Let Him use your situation to do His work. Let it go. Stop trying frantically to hold it together. Surrender to brokenness.

When God's Word is planted in a broken heart—a prepared heart—it produces a crop of wisdom, insight, and understanding. But what was sown "'on good soil is the man who hears the word and understands it. He produces a crop, yielding a hundred, sixty or thirty times what was sown'" (Matt. 13:23). What do you think would be the deciding factor in whether a seed brought forth a thirtyfold increase or a sixtyfold increase or a hundredfold increase? I think it would be the condition of the ground. Can you be satisfied with a thirtyfold increase or a sixtyfold increase if you know that a hundredfold increase is possible?

- Where does your heart need to be plowed to receive the Word of God and see it produce a hundredfold crop? Listen to the Father and write down what He says.

_____

_____

_____

- Where is your flesh standing in the way of what God wants to do in you?

_____

_____

_____

- Will you trust God's love, purposes, and power enough to surrender this situation to Him and let it produce brokenness in you? If you will, you will find rest for your soul.

_____

_____

Celebration

Write down one thought from your retreat time today about God's character or His work that awes you. What did He seem to highlight for you? Let that thought be the focus of your worship and celebration. Carry your celebration into your day.

_____

~ Day 3 ~

Centering

Begin with centering prayer. Close your eyes and mentally move yourself into His presence. See Him with the eyes of your heart. Let this scriptural thought form the basis of your experience: "As the deer pants for streams of water, / so my soul pants for you, O God" (Ps. 42:1).

Meditation

"I have been crucified with Christ and I no longer live,
but Christ lives in me." (Gal. 2:20)

With these words, Paul declared his "old man," the Paul-centered person he used to be, dead. His flesh-based dependence on his own strength had been broken, so the life flowing through him was the life of Christ. Paul's mind, will, and emotions (soul) had now become the conduits through which the living Jesus expressed Himself. Because his outer man had been broken, Paul's personality and intellect and passions could be what they were always meant to be: receptacles to contain and dispense the power of the Spirit. His brokenness became the entryway into a life of spiritual power.

Again we are brought face-to-face with the fact that brokenness is a prerequisite for experiencing the fullness of the Spirit's power. Again we are reminded that brokenness is not to be avoided or feared because its product is wholeness. How does God do this breaking? Scripture points us to the crucifixion: "'I have been crucified with Christ.'" Our old nature must pass through a crucifixion.

Does it seem to you that certain situations repeatedly bring out the same reactions in you every time? Do you often find yourself repeating destructive behavior patterns? Do you find that numerous situations arouse in you a familiar emotion like anger, fear, envy, or shame?

When we react in the flesh, it is the tendency of our human nature to blame circumstances or to blame the people around us. You may be able to pinpoint an outside cause, but that outside cause is not the ultimate source. God is always in the process of breaking the patterns established by your flesh. He allows you to be confronted with the same weakness over and over again. See these incidents for what they are: crucifixion moments.

At a crucifixion moment you are offered two choices: to react in the old way of your human nature or to react in the new way of the Spirit. When you choose to place blame on others or feel martyred by circumstances beyond your control, you resuscitate your self-life. When, on the other hand, you choose to look away from the outside cause and accept the crucifying work of the Spirit, you begin, little-by-little, to let the old nature die and the new nature emerge.

Crucifixion is voluntary. Jesus, whose crucifixion is our model, said, "'No one takes [my life] from me, but I lay it down of my own accord'" (John 10:18). Every time you are confronted with a crucifixion moment, choose to lay down your self-life. Choose to surrender your pride, your expectations, your rights, your demands. Choose the way of the cross. Let someone else get the credit you deserve; forgo the opportunity to have the last word; die to the demands of your flesh.

The spiritual power which surfaces is resurrection power. The life that bears the marks of death is resurrection life. Only that which is eternal can pass through death and come forth alive. Resurrection life is eternal life—life from which the limitations imposed by flesh have been left in the grave. When everything that can be destroyed has been destroyed, then you come to know the power of an indestructible life (Heb. 7:16; 12:27–28). When you surrender yourself to crucifixion, you can be assured that resurrection will follow. The Spirit of Him who raised Jesus from the dead will express that very power through you (Rom. 8:11).

Brokenness! What a beautiful word.

- Do you recognize crucifixion moments that you have been resisting? What are they? What sin-pattern are they exposing?

_____

_____

_____

- Right now, will you accept these crucifixion moments as ultimately coming from the Father? Acknowledge that He is allowing them for His redemptive and restorative purposes. Write out your honest feelings about your crucifixion moments. Remember that God is not fragile and His love for you is not dependent on your having "acceptable" feelings. You can be brutally and fearlessly honest with Him.

_____

_____

_____

Celebration

Write down one thought from your retreat time today about God's character or His work that awes you. What did He seem to highlight for you? Let that thought be the focus of your worship and celebration. Carry your celebration into your day.

_____

~ Day 4 ~

Centering

Begin with centering prayer. Close your eyes and mentally move yourself into His presence. See Him with the eyes of your heart. Let this scriptural thought form the basis of your experience: "Show me your face / let me hear your voice; / for your voice is sweet, / and your face is lovely" (Song of Sol. 2:14).

Meditation

"He must become greater; I must become less." (John 3:30)

- Read Mark 14:3–9.

- What did the woman in these verses bring to Jesus? What did she intend to do with it?

_____

_____

- What did she have to do to be able to pour out the perfume?

_____

_____

The woman brought with her an alabaster jar of very expensive perfume. Her gift had two elements: precious content and costly packaging. Not only was the perfume expensive, so was the alabaster jar that held it. Because of its value, this alabaster jar of perfume may have been passed down from generation to generation, unopened and unused. The only way to open the alabaster jar was to break it. It had no twist-off lid or reclosable top. The only way for the perfume to be released was for the alabaster jar—the costly, precious, expensive jar—to be destroyed. Once destroyed, that valuable packaging could not be reassembled. You might say that the packaging had to die so that the perfume could be dispersed.

You and I, the packaging designed by God to contain the fragrance of the Son, are disposable. We must not place so much value on the packaging that the content is never dispersed. If my outward expression, that which others define as "Jennifer," takes priority over the substance, the life for whom I am but a container, then Jesus will not express His radical self through me. If I am too enamored by the packaging, I will not let it die so that Jesus can have supremacy.

When the outside packaging is cherished and safeguarded, the inside is kept hidden. The content may never be poured out to the world if the vessel is given too much significance.

A *vessel* is an object that exists for one reason: to be a receptacle for something else. Scripture says we are the vessels to contain the Son's life. Christ fills us. Then He pours Himself out into my world through me, and into your world through you. Your surrendered life makes His ministry available to those in your world. God's all-surpassing power is poured out through jars of clay (2 Cor. 4:7).

We are only the containers for His power.

I may say to a glove, "Glove, pick up this Bible," and yet, somehow, the glove cannot do it. It has got a thumb and fingers, the shape and form of a hand, and yet it is unable to do the thing I command it to do. You may say, "Well, of course not. You have never told the glove how!" But I may preach to and instruct that glove until my patience is exhausted, but the glove, try as it will, still cannot pick up that Bible. Yet I have a glove at home that has picked up my Bible dozens of times!—but never once before I put my hand into it! As soon, however, as my hand comes into that glove, the glove becomes as strong as my hand. Everything possible to my hand becomes possible to that glove—but only in the measure in which the glove is prepared simply to clothe the activity of the hand.[14]

Major Thomas's picture of a glove filled with the life of a hand illustrates a believer filled with the life of Christ. The glove has no life in itself, but it was created to contain and express life. *When I fill a glove with my hand, the glove is transformed into the image of my hand.* Everything my hand does, it does through the glove, but the focus is my hand, not the glove. If I were to shake your hand while wearing my glove, you would not say, "I shook Jennifer Dean's glove." You would say, "I shook Jennifer Dean's hand." Whatever comes into contact with my glove has come into contact with my hand. My hand expresses itself through the glove. The glove is only strong when it yields itself to the indwelling hand.

You could reason, "Apart from the hand, the glove can do nothing"; but "the glove can do everything through the hand that gives it strength." Furthermore, "He has given the glove life, and this life is in the hand. The glove that has the hand has life; the glove that does not have the hand does not have life" (paraphrase of John 15:5; Phil. 4:13; 1 John 5:11–12).

As I relinquish my human, limited, self-involved will to God's divine, eternal, all-knowing will, I begin to act as He acts. As I decrease so that He can increase, I become the vessel through which He operates.

My brokenness releases His fullness.

- We all have a concept of how we want others to perceive us. We have developed "packaging"—ways of presenting ourselves—that matches that concept. This is not wrong in itself. It becomes a hindrance when it takes on too high a value. Be honest in describing how you want others to see you.

_____

_____

_____

- In what ways are you valuing your packaging more than your content—the life of Christ in you? What do you need to do to break open the packaging and release the fragrance?

_____

_____

_____

Celebration

Write down one thought from your retreat time today about God's character or His work that awes you. What did He seem to highlight for you? Let that thought be the focus of your worship and celebration. Carry your celebration into your day.

_____

~ Day 5 ~

Centering

Begin with centering prayer. Close your eyes and mentally move yourself into His presence. See Him with the eyes of your heart. Let this scriptural thought form the basis of your experience: "'Surely God is my salvation; / I will trust and not be afraid. / The LORD, the LORD is my strength and my song; / he has become my salvation'" (Isa. 12:2).

Meditation

And he took bread, . . . and broke it, and gave it to them, saying, "This is my body." (Luke 22:19)

His body, the physical vessel that temporarily contained His life, was broken so the life it housed could be made available to dwell in you and me. His willingness to be broken makes it possible for us to be whole.

The Old Testament pictured this brokenness when the priests of the old covenant were consecrated and set apart. Part of their ceremony was to bring a grain offering, made into cakes and broken in pieces.

> "This is the offering Aaron and his sons are to bring to the LORD on the day he is anointed: a tenth of an ephah of fine flour as a regular grain offering, half of it in the morning and half in the evening. Prepare it with oil on a griddle; bring it well-mixed and *present the grain offering broken in pieces as an aroma pleasing to the LORD.*"(Lev. 6:20–21, italics added)

This broken offering pleased the Lord. The flour and oil mixture, a type of bread, represented the body of Jesus, and it also represented the flesh (soul apart from God's indwelling power) of God's people. Our outer person, our flesh or our self-centeredness, must be broken to release spiritual power from Christ within. The unbroken flesh is what hinders Jesus from being all-powerful within us.

He allowed His body to be broken for you. Will you allow your flesh to be broken for Him?

He endured the savagery of the crucifixion by His own free will, because He knew that the glory it would bring outweighed the pain it would cost. "Let us fix our eyes on Jesus, the author and perfecter of our faith, who *for the joy set before him* endured the cross, scorning its shame, and sat down at the right hand of the throne of God" (Heb. 12:2, italics added). The hope of brokenness rests in the joy set before you: Crucifixion always gives way to resurrection.

> Little-by-little we are changed by this daily crucifixion of the will. Changed, not like a tornado changes things, but like a grain of sand in an oyster changes things. . . . Please remember, we are dealing with the crucifixion of the will, not the obliteration of the will. Crucifixion always has resurrection tied to it. God is not destroying the will but transforming it so that over a process of time and experience we can freely will what God wills.[15]

Do you long to live in the Spirit's present-tense power? Do you want to know the indwelling life of Christ as your reality instead of an empty theology? Do you want Jesus to fill you with Himself? Do you want the living Lord to be someone you know, not just someone you believe in? Then embrace brokenness.

- Do you feel satisfied that you are experiencing all that God has for you every day? In what ways?

_____

_____

_____

• Do you believe that God has more power available than you have yet experienced? Why or why not?

_____

_____

_____

• Respond to what the Spirit brings to your mind in answer to this question: What are you willing to do or what changes are you willing to make to release His power in your life?

_____

_____

_____

Celebration

Write down one thought from your retreat time today about God's character or His work that awes you. What did He seem to highlight for you? Let that thought be the focus of your worship and celebration. Carry your celebration into your day.

_____

Review and Reflect

- In your own words, define *brokenness.*

_____

_____

_____

- What does brokenness specifically mean in your life right now?

_____

_____

_____

- Before this week's meditations, what did the word *brokenness* mean to you? How did you feel about it?

_____

_____

_____

- What has changed this week in your feelings about brokenness?

_____

_____

_____

• What does this verse mean to you?
  "I have been crucified with Christ and I no longer live, but Christ lives in me." (Gal. 2:20)

  _____

  _____

  _____

• What is a "crucifixion moment"?

  _____

  _____

  _____

• Describe some crucifixion moments in your history and what they have produced in your life.

  _____

  _____

  _____

• Are you confronted with a crucifixion moment right now? What are your feelings about it?

  _____

  _____

  _____

~ Day 7 ~

Journal Your Thoughts and Prayers

_____

_____

_____

_____

_____

_____

_____

_____

_____

_____

_____

_____

_____

_____

_____

_____

_____

_____

_____

_____

_____

_____

_____

_____

_____

_____

_____

_____

_____

_____

_____

_____

_____

_____

_____

_____

_____

_____

_____

_____

_____

_____

_____

_____

_____

WEEK 2

A New Heart

> *"'I will give them a heart to know me,*
> *that I am the LORD.'" (Jer. 24:7)*

His life—everything about Him—is operating *in you* by resurrection power. As He reproduces in you His own pure heart, your heart cries, "I have come not to do my will, but to do the will of Him who sent me."

~ Day 8 ~

Centering

Begin with centering prayer. Let the Spirit usher you into the presence of the Father. Take time to experience His pleasure and His delight in you. Let Him make His Word real for you: "'The LORD your God is with you, / . . . He will take great delight in you, / he will quiet you with his love, / he will rejoice over you with singing'" (Zeph. 3:17).

Meditation

*"'I will put my law in their minds
and write it on their hearts.'" (Jer. 31:33)*

Just as new life sprouts from a seed that has fallen into the ground to die, so new life emerges from a heart that has surrendered to crucifixion. The heart that has yielded to the death-work of the Spirit by offering up its flesh for execution begins to experience the power of the cross. The power of the cross lies in the fact that when the flesh is broken, the Spirit is released. Fully accomplished crucifixion gives way to resurrection. "We always carry around in our body the death of Jesus, so that the life of Jesus may also be revealed in our body. For we who are alive are always being given over to death for Jesus' sake, so that his life may be revealed in our mortal body" (2 Cor. 4:10–11). Let death work so life can be revealed. Let the Father give you a new heart, full of resurrection power.

What does God say about this new heart that now pumps resurrection life? It is the tablet upon which He has written His thoughts. ""'I will put my law in their minds / and write it on their hearts'"" (Jer. 31:33). The new heart is a clean slate, available for the finger of God to write on it His will and His desires. When the Father first revealed His holiness by defining His standard of righteousness, the finger of God wrote it on tablets of stone (Exod. 31:18). When the Father imparts His holiness to His people, He

Himself engraves it on their hearts. His holiness and His presence become their deepest desire. Indelibly He has carved into the spirit-core of His crucified and resurrected ones the single truth through which all facts are filtered: I *am* the Lord. """I will give them a heart to know me, that I am the LORD"" (Jer. 24:7).

Your heart knows Him and recognizes Him. Jesus said, "'I know my sheep and my sheep know me—just as the Father knows me and I know the Father'" (John 10:14–15). You know in a deep, visceral, intuitive way that He is the Lord.

- Do you recognize that the reason you long for holiness is because the Father has written it on your heart? Write out your longing for Him and His righteousness.

- What external behaviors contradict your inner longing for holiness? In other words, what sin has entangled you?

- What do you think is the root of that sin? Is it pride? Is it self-indulgence? What flesh-life still needs to go to the cross?

- Write what the Spirit has named for you in the blank and make this your faith declaration: "_____ *is crucified with Christ and* _____ *no longer lives. Christ is now expressing His resurrection power where* _____ *once held power.*"

Celebration

Let the Spirit remind you of what you know about the power of God. Dwell on the fact that His power is at work *in you,* accomplishing more than you can ask or imagine (Eph. 3:20). Let this thought be the focus of your worship and celebration.

~ $\mathcal{D}_{ay}$ 9 ~

Centering

Begin with centering prayer. Let the Spirit usher you into the presence of the Father. Take time to experience His pleasure and His delight in you. Let Him make His Word real for you: "'The LORD be exalted, / who delights in the well-being of his servant'" (Ps. 35:27).

Meditation

Surely you desire truth in the inner parts;
you teach me wisdom in the inmost place. (Ps. 51:6)

What the physical heart is to the body, the spiritual heart is to the soul. It is the "inner part" and the "inmost place," the point from which all life flows. The physical heart propels blood for life through the body. Without a sound, strong heart, blood is not effectively dispersed to blood-starved cells. From the spiritual heart flows the spiritual power that imparts life to the soul. Truth and wisdom are the components of a healthy spirit-heart. The person whose flesh-life has been crucified will experience the natural and spontaneous flow of truth and wisdom. Truth and wisdom are not disciplines or courses of study, but ever-flowing life (Col. 2:2–3). No longer striving for holiness by the power of the flesh, this person finds holiness springing up within as a river of life.

Truth, wisdom, and holiness all have one definition: Jesus. He is the truth. He is the wisdom of God. He is holiness. His life flowing through the spirit-veins of a person dispenses truth from the inner parts and wisdom from the inmost being. The new heart pumps new life. His thoughts flow into our minds. His emotions flow into our emotions. His will flows into our wills. He floods our souls with Himself.

Disobedience—yielding to the flesh—disrupts the flow. Just like tying a tourniquet around a part of the body stops the flow of blood to that body part, disobedience stops the flow of His life through us.[16]

Another way to describe the effect of disobedience is that it produces a callous heart. Scripture warns against a heart that has become callous (Isa. 6:10; Matt. 13:15; Acts 28:27). A callus develops progressively as skin repeatedly comes into contact with a foreign object. The callus develops to protect the skin's nerve endings from being sensitive to the irritant. God says that when our flesh repeatedly comes into contact with His Spirit and disobeys His voice, a callus develops over our hearts and they become progressively less sensitive to Him. "'Today, if you hear his voice, / do not harden your hearts'" (Heb. 3:15). The word translated *hear* means to hear and respond in one action. When you hear and do not respond, your heart begins to form a callus.

When the Spirit of God confronts and exposes your flesh, offer it up to Him as a living sacrifice. Do not resist Him. Keep your heart free of flesh and calluses so that truth and wisdom will circulate freely through you and so that your heart will be sensitive to the Spirit's every word.

- Is there truth in your inner parts and wisdom in your inmost being? Are truth and wisdom your driving force? Or do your actions spring from your flesh?

  _____

  _____

- Is your flesh coming into contact with God's voice? Will you resist Him and allow a callus to continue growing over your heart? Or will you yield to His work in you, allowing Him to slough away the callus?

  _____

  _____

Celebration

Let the Spirit remind you of what you know about the power of God. Dwell on the fact that His power is at work *in you,* accomplishing more than you can ask or imagine (Eph. 3:20). Let this thought be the focus of your worship and celebration.

~ *Day 10* ~

Centering

Begin with centering prayer. Let the Spirit usher you into the presence of the Father. Take time to experience His pleasure and His delight in you. Let Him make His Word real for you: "They feast on the abundance of your house; / you give them drink from your river of delights" (Ps. 36:8).

Meditation

The blood of Jesus, his Son, purifies us from all sin. . . .
If we confess our sins, he is faithful and just and will
forgive us our sins and purify us from all unrighteousness.
(1 John 1:7, 9)

The Father is purifying His people. He is actively, aggressively cleansing them from the inside out. Jesus said that when the inside is clean, the outside will also be clean (Matt. 23:26). His work is focused on the heart. He is creating for Himself a clean-hearted people. He is cleansing *your* heart. A heart that is clean produces behavior that is holy.

How is He doing His cleansing work? How is He purging His people from the unrighteous nature that gives birth to sin? He is doing it by the blood of the Son. "The blood of Jesus, his Son, purifies us from all sin" (1 John 1:7). God will not only forgive our sins—delete them from our record—but He will also purify us from the unrighteousness that caused the sin (1 John 1:9). Both of these things He will do by the blood of His Son. In fact, the verb tense used in the Greek tells us that this cleansing by the blood is an ongoing action. He is continuously cleansing us from all unrighteousness by the blood of the Son. When John wrote that God will "purify us from all unrighteousness," he did not mean that we will attain sinless perfection while still in our earthly bodies. He meant that no form of unrighteousness is outside the scope of God's power to cleanse. We will become more and more purified each day. We will come closer and closer to being completely free from unrighteousness. No sin is impossible for God to root out.

How does blood cleanse? It cleanses as it flows. It does not cleanse by being applied externally, but by flowing through the veins in a ceaseless, cleansing fountain. The life of Jesus flows through your spirit-veins like blood flows through your body, like the vine's life flows through the branch. By His resurrection life operating in you, you are continually and progressively being made pure, "being transformed into his likeness, with everincreasing glory" (2 Cor. 3:18).

As blood flows through your body, its red cells absorb toxins and transport them to the organs through which they will be expelled. As blood flows through your body, it brings oxygen and nutrients that give new life to your cells. Your physical blood is actively and continuously bringing new life. As it flows through your body, old things are passing away; new things are coming. As His life flows through you like blood flows through your body, it is bringing His life-giving, sin-cleansing power to flush away spiritual toxins and deliver resurrection life (Rom. 6:4; 2 Cor. 5:17).

He is purifying you, making you new on the inside. He is giving you a new heart, a heart through which the life of His Son flows. He is doing a perpetual cleansing, bringing about an ever-increasing purity of the heart.

- Focus on this thought: *The life of the Son is flowing through me.*

- As you view your life through that truth, what does it mean to you in practical terms? What difference does it make?

_____

_____

- In what aspects of your life do you see an ever-increasing purity being expressed?

_____

_____

Celebration

Let the Spirit remind you of what you know about the power of God. Dwell on the fact that His power is at work *in you,* accomplishing more than you can ask or imagine (Eph. 3:20). Let this thought be the focus of your worship and celebration.

~ Day 11 ~

Centering

Begin with centering prayer. Let the Spirit usher you into the presence of the Father. Take time to experience His pleasure and His delight in you. Let Him make His Word real for you: "As a bridegroom rejoices over his bride, / so will your God rejoice over you" (Isa. 62:5).

Meditation

Cleanse me with hyssop, and I will be clean;
wash me, and I will be whiter than snow. (Ps. 51:7)

The Father Himself must do the cleansing. The Father Himself gave you a heart to know Him. *He* inscribed His desires and thoughts on your new heart. *He* will cleanse your heart and keep it clean. The psalmist's meaning is, "If *You* cleanse me, then I will be clean. If *You* wash me, then I will be whiter than snow."

Visualize a clear glass. Do you see it? Now imagine that glass filled with dirty, nasty water. Look closely and see the dirt particles floating in the water. See how cloudy it is? A layer of scum glazes the top and sediment has settled on the bottom.

Now pour the water out of the glass. When the dirty water is gone, what remains? Is the glass clean? No, the dirt clings to the sides. The sediment may be rearranged, but it's still there. What will happen when you put clean water into the glass? The water will pick up the dirt on the glass and the clean water will be contaminated.

Let that picture represent for you the effect of self-effort to produce purity in yourself. No matter how hard you try, you cannot make yourself pure.

Revisualize your glass full of dirty water. This time, put the glass under a faucet and turn on the water. Now watch what happens. The continual flow of fresh, clean water begins to push out the old dirty water. Eventually, the force of the flow even disturbs the sediment on the bottom and washes it out. Finally, the glass is clean—it's filled with clean water, and clean water is spilling over the edges.

What's the secret? The fresh and continual flow of water.

> "If anyone is thirsty, let him come to me and drink. . . . streams of living water will flow from within him." (John 7:37–38)

How can you open your life to the Father's ongoing cleansing? By being engaged in a continual interaction with the living and indwelling Jesus.

- Read Jeremiah 24:7. At whose initiative do you have a heart that recognizes the Lord?

  _____

  _____

- Read Ezekiel 36:26–27. At whose initiative do you have a new heart and new spirit? At whose initiative will you be motivated to walk in His ways?

  _____

  _____

- Read 2 Corinthians 3:18. Whose work produces ever-increasing Christlikeness?

  _____

  _____

- Take time to recognize and yield to His work in you. If He has taken the initiative and the full responsibility for producing what He desires in you, then do you believe He is able to do what He has set out to do? Read Romans 4:20–21 and Philippians 1:6.

Celebration

Let the Spirit remind you of what you know about the power of God. Dwell on the fact that His power is at work *in you,* accomplishing more than you can ask or imagine (Eph. 3:20). Let this thought be the focus of your worship and celebration.

~ Day 12 ~

Centering

Begin with centering prayer. Let the Spirit usher you into the presence of the Father. Take the time to experience His pleasure and His delight in you. Let Him make His Word real for you: "'I will rejoice in doing them good and will assuredly plant them in this land with all my heart and soul'" (Jer. 32:41).

Meditation

"For I have come down from heaven not to do my will
but to do the will of him who sent me." (John 6:38)

Søren Kierkegaard said, "Purity of heart is to will one thing." The word *pure* means "unmixed, unalloyed, containing nothing extraneous." A pure heart is one from which all flesh has been cut away. A pure heart is one that has been united with Christ in His crucifixion and also united with Him in His resurrection (Rom. 6:5). It has submitted flesh-life to the Spirit's deathblows so that spiritual power can emerge. The pure heart wills one thing: to do the will of the Father.

When we offer our flesh to be crucified, what is it that dies? Our will dies. Our desire to receive the proper recognition, to pay back a wrong, to gratify our egos, or to satisfy any of the many flesh-born yearnings dies a painful, savage death of crucifixion. As we allow our flesh to be broken and to die, the life of Christ flowing through us becomes our life. His life—everything about Him—is operating *in you* by resurrection power. As He reproduces in you His own pure heart, your heart cries, "I have come not to do my will, but to do the will of Him who sent me."

Because the Father has written His will on our hearts, in reality His will is our deepest desire. "'I desire to do your will, O my God; / your law is within my heart'" (Ps. 40:8). "Direct me in the path of your commands, /

for there I find delight" (Ps. 119:35). A purified, cleansed, flesh-free heart has found its home.

- Where are there conflicts in your life right now? Perhaps they are emotional conflicts; perhaps relational conflicts.

  _____

  _____

- In each area of conflict, what is your flesh desiring? What is the Spirit of God desiring?

  _____

  _____

- Take each conflict to the cross. Surrender your flesh for crucifixion. Align yourself with God's will and turn your back on what your flesh desires. To help give you a tangible way to see the spiritual transaction you are making, try this: Draw a picture of the cross and write on it each situation, relationship, sin, or flesh-pattern you are surrendering to the cross. Embrace the resurrection that follows, even if you don't feel it immediately.

Celebration

Let the Spirit remind you of what you know about the power of God. Dwell on the fact that His power is at work *in you,* accomplishing more than you can ask or imagine (Eph. 3:20). Let this thought be the focus of your worship and celebration.

Review and Reflect

- In your own words, what is a pure heart?

  _____

  _____

  _____

- Where does a pure heart come from?

  _____

  _____

  _____

- What do you think are some of the characteristics of a pure heart?

  _____

  _____

  _____

- Why is a pure heart desirable?

  _____

  _____

  _____

• What will a pure heart cost you?

_____

_____

_____

• What does this verse mean to you?

"'I will give you a new heart and put a new spirit in you; I will remove from you your heart of stone and give you a heart of flesh. And I will put my Spirit in you and move you to follow my decrees and be careful to keep my laws.'" (Ezek. 36:26–27)

_____

_____

_____

Journal Your Thoughts and Prayers

_____

_____

_____

_____

_____

_____

_____

_____

_____

_____

_____

_____

_____

_____

_____

_____

_____

_____

_____

WEEK 3

An Undivided Heart

"I will give them an undivided heart and put a new spirit in them." (Ezek. 11:19)

God engineered your salvation not only for the purpose of cleansing you of sin but also for the purpose of filling you with Himself. The work He is doing—the breaking, the crucifying, the cleansing—all has one purpose: to prepare His chosen dwelling place for His presence.

~ Day 15 ~

Centering

Begin with centering prayer. Focus your thoughts on the truth of God's presence. In the inner sanctuary of your soul, take a position of worship. Let this be your heart's cry: "The LORD is my light and my salvation— / whom shall I fear? / The Lord is the stronghold of my life— / of whom shall I be afraid?" (Ps. 27:1).

Meditation

Teach me your way, O LORD,
and I will walk in your truth;
give me an undivided heart,
that I may fear your name. (Ps. 86:11)

Focus is essential for success in any area. To choose one goal means to dismiss many other possible goals. The person who has focused his or her mind, emotions, and energy on a single goal is the one who stands out from the crowd. The goal becomes the filter through which he or she evaluates all options. A goal-focused person knows this: If it does not, on some level, move me closer to my goal, then it distracts me from my goal. A goal-focused person has an undivided heart.

Jesus described an undivided heart. "'Love the Lord your God with all your heart and with all your soul and with all your mind and with all your strength'" (Mark 12:30). The heart focused on the Father has no room for anything but Him. When we have allowed the Spirit to clear away all the clutter and rubble from our hearts, then He can fill them with His glory, just as He filled the tabernacle with His glory (Exod. 40:34).

God engineered your salvation not only for the purpose of cleansing you of sin but also for the purpose of filling you with Himself. The work He is doing—the breaking, the crucifying, the cleansing—all has one purpose: to prepare His chosen dwelling place for His presence.

Just as in the days of Hezekiah, when the priests removed every unclean thing from the temple to make it fit for the Lord (2 Chron. 29:16), so the Spirit of God is removing all unrighteousness and all flesh to make room for the presence of the Lord in your heart. He must be your heart's only inhabitant. "'I will not yield my glory to another'" (Isa. 48:11). What God instructed the priests through Hezekiah is your instruction: "Carry the uncleanness out from the holy place" (2 Chron. 29:5, NASB). He will not share His dwelling place. He will inhabit it alone.

You were created to be His home, the place where His glory dwells. In the Old Testament, the temple is a multilayered shadow of spiritual truth. It is a picture of Jesus, foretelling His death, burial, and resurrection life. It is also the picture of each believer. You and I are the temple. He numbers you among those who have been "'called by my name, / whom I created for my glory, / whom I formed and made'" (Isa. 43:7). He calls *you* by His own name; He created *you* for His glory; He formed *you* and made *you.*

In the Old Testament picture, His glory was manifested in the tabernacle, and later the temple. The temple was created for His glory. Your soul filled with His life is the reality foreshadowed and pictured by the temple. You are created to be His glory. The word translated *glory* means "the true expression of something." Your soul is to be so filled with Him and so free from flesh that it is His glory—an accurate expression of Him. He is removing uncleanness from your heart so that He can fill it with His presence. He is preparing for Himself an undivided heart.

- Read Psalm 86:11. What prefaces David's request for an undivided heart? Write out the opening prayer of this verse.

_____

_____

_____

- How does praying, "Teach me your way, . . . and I will walk in your truth" prepare the way for also praying, "Give me an undivided heart, that I may fear your name"?

_____

_____

_____

- Do you find that the more you know of God's truth, the more you truly desire it? The more you understand His ways, the more you long to be free from the ways of the flesh? "I gain understanding from your precepts; / therefore I hate every wrong path" (Ps. 119:104). Write out your thoughts.

_____

_____

_____

Celebration

Worship and celebrate. Contemplate the fact that the glory of God is filling you. He says of you, His dwelling place, ""'I myself will be a wall of fire around it,' declares the LORD, 'and I will be its glory within'"" (Zech. 2:5). Let this thought fill you with wonder.

~ Day 16 ~

Centering

Begin with centering prayer. Focus your thoughts on the truth of God's presence. In the inner sanctuary of your soul, take a position of worship. Let this be your heart's cry: "Many, O LORD my God, / are the wonders you have done. / The things you planned for us / no one can recount to you; / were I to speak and tell of them, / they would be too many to declare" (Ps. 40:5).

Meditation

He will have no fear of bad news;
his heart is steadfast, trusting in the LORD. (Ps. 112:7)

A righteous person, claimed the psalmist, will have a steadfast heart. *Webster's Dictionary* defines *steadfast* as "firmly fixed in place; immovable; not subject to change." Focused. Undivided.

Once your heart has been filled with His presence, it is anchored in Him. No longer are you "like a wave of the sea, blown and tossed by the wind" (James 1:6). You are steady. You have come to rest in Him. This is His goal in freeing you of your flesh. The flesh cannot put its full trust in God because the flesh's whole way of operating is trust in self. The flesh is the natural enemy of the Spirit. It is, by its nature, hostile to God and unable to submit to Him (Rom. 8:6–8). Flesh cannot be rehabilitated or purified. It must be crucified. It must be cut off. The heart must be circumcised of flesh. "In him you were also circumcised, in the putting off of the sinful nature, not with a circumcision done by the hands of men but with the circumcision done by Christ" (Col. 2:11).

In Psalm 112:7, the psalmist defined a steadfast heart as "trusting in the LORD." Trust is all or nothing. You trust or you don't trust. Humans function by actively trusting. Because we cannot control our environment, we have to trust in order to function. Every move a human being makes is, in some degree, an act of trust. At the most mundane levels of living, trust is so ingrained that we don't even think about it. For example, every time I enter a building, I am actively trusting that it won't collapse around me. But I don't think about that trust. Do you see? Trust is operating in you all the time.

Underlying it all, every person has a focus for his or her faith. Either he or she trusts in the flesh or trusts in the Lord. Scripture describes the difference between the two.

> This is what the LORD says:
> "Cursed is the one who trusts in man,
>   who depends on flesh for his strength
>   and whose heart turns away from the LORD.
> He will be like a bush in the wastelands;
>   he will not see prosperity when it comes.
> He will dwell in the parched places of the desert,
>   in a salt land where no one lives.
> But blessed is the man who trusts in the LORD,
>   whose confidence is in him.
> He will be like a tree planted by the water
>   that sends out its roots by the stream.
> It does not fear when heat comes;
>   its leaves are always green.
> It has no worries in a year of drought
>   and never fails to bear fruit." (Jer. 17:5–8)

The steadfast heart has settled its trust in God. A steadfast heart is a heart at rest. A steadfast heart is at home in the Father and the Father is at home in the steadfast heart. It is a place of quiet confidence. Steady. Sure. Safe.

Do you see that the brokenness that God is bringing into your life has a purpose? He is emptying you of your flesh in order to fill you with Himself. He is cleansing you of sin in order to make room for His glory. He is in the process of giving you a steadfast, undivided heart to replace your old, unsteady, unreliable heart. The process has some pain inherent in it, but when you recognize that the pain is a means to an end, it takes on a new meaning. Get that end resolutely in focus.

I like the way Colossians 2:9 describes the goal: "For in Christ all the fullness of the Deity lives in bodily form, and you have been given fullness in Christ." In other words, Christ is full of God and you are full of Christ. Live that fullness.

- Read Psalm 112:7. Describe a steadfast heart.

_____

_____

- Why will a steadfast heart have no fear of bad news?

_____

_____

- What do you believe this statement means: "For the person who is fully surrendered to God and His purposes, good is good, and bad is also good"? Do you believe this?

_____

_____

_____

- In your life, what is troubling you right now?

_____

_____

_____

- How is it exposing your flesh-life? Why is that good?

_____

_____

_____

Celebration

Worship and celebrate. Contemplate the fact that the glory of God is filling you. He says of you, His dwelling place, ""'I myself will be a wall of fire around it," declares the LORD, "and I will be its glory within"'" (Zech. 2:5). Let this thought fill you with wonder.

~ Day 17 ~

Centering

Begin with centering prayer. Focus your thoughts on the truth of God's presence. In the inner sanctuary of your soul, take a position of worship. Let this be your heart's cry: "I have set the LORD always before me. / Because he is at my right hand, / I will not be shaken. / Therefore my heart is glad and my tongue rejoices; / my body also will rest secure" (Ps. 16:8–9).

Meditation

"You will keep in perfect peace
him whose mind is steadfast,
because he trusts in you." (Isa. 26:3)

A steadfast heart experiences uninterrupted peace. Perfect peace. Its undercurrent of peace is not interrupted when bad news comes, nor does it live with the fear that bad news will come. The steadfast heart has been set free from fear because it knows the truth. A person whose heart is steadfast knows that God is *always* in control; no matter what form circumstances take, He is working everything out for His purposes. The person whose heart is steadfast trusts "him who works out everything in conformity with the purpose of his will" (Eph. 1:11).

The psalmist wrote in Psalm 112:7, "His heart is steadfast, trusting in the LORD." The same thought is expressed in Isaiah 26:3: "You will keep in perfect peace / him whose mind is steadfast, / because he trusts in you." An active trust in the Lord is the cornerstone of a steadfast heart. It is the Lord and His perfect faithfulness, His trustworthiness, that imparts steadfastness to a heart. The trust of which Scripture speaks is not an emotion or a doctrine, but a way of living in which every thought, every word, and every act is an expression of total dependence upon the Father. The righteous *live* by faith. Faith is not something that you get out and dust off when things are bad; faith is not a currency you trade in for favors from God. For your spiritual life, faith is the air in your lungs and the blood in your veins; it is the active ingredient in your spiritual composition.

The model of a steadfast heart is Jesus. The model of living by faith is Jesus. The model of a mind kept in perfect peace is Jesus. What is the secret He modeled for us? To what did He attribute His steadfastness?

> "I tell you the truth, the Son can do nothing by himself, he can do only what he sees his Father doing, because whatever the Father does the Son also does. For the Father loves the Son and shows him all he does." (John 5:19–20)

> "I do nothing on my own but speak just what the Father has taught me." (John 8:28)

> "Don't you believe that I am in the Father, and that the Father is in me? The words I say to you are not just my own. Rather, it is the Father, living in me, who is doing his work." (John 14:10)

Time and time again Jesus explained the reason for His power and His peace. In everything He said and everything He did, Jesus was the vehicle for the activity of the Father who lived in Him. His heart was undivided. He willed one thing. He lived for no other reason but to do God's will.

Perhaps you're thinking, "Yes, but that was Jesus. I'm not Jesus." It's true that you and I are not Jesus. But Scripture shows us that we are to be related to Jesus in the same way that Jesus was related to the Father; we are to interact with Jesus in the same way that Jesus interacted with the Father.

Let me paraphrase what Jesus said. "I love you the very same way the Father loves Me (John 15:9). Because the Father loves Me, He shows Me everything He's doing (John 5:20); because I love you, I'll show you everything I'm doing (John 15:15; 14:21). You are to obey Me the same way that I obey the Father. I obey the Father by allowing Him to do His work through Me, by being fully surrendered to the power of His life flowing through Me (John 14:10–11). If you obey Me the same way I obey the Father, you'll have the same kind of relationship with Me that I have with the Father—the Father is in Me and I am in the Father (John 14:10; 17:21); in the same way, I am in you (John 17:23; Gal. 2:20) and you are in Me (Eph. 1:20; Col. 3:3). Do you see how I live securely in My Father's love? Do you see how My heart is steadfast, trusting in Him? You will live the same way, trusting in Me."

Jesus' Relationship to the Father	Your Relationship to Jesus
"The Son can do nothing by himself." (John 5:19)	Apart from me, you can do nothing." (John 15:5)
"The Father . . . shows him all he does." (John 5:20)	"I too will . . . show myself to him." (John 14:21)
	"Everything that I learned from my Father I have made known to you." (John 15:15)
"I am in the Father, and . . . the Father is in me." (John 14:10)	"If a man remains in me and I in him. . . ." (John 15:5)
"The Son [will] bring glory to the Father." (John 14:13)	"Glory has come to me through them." (John 17:10)
"The Father knows me and I know the Father." (John 10:15)	"I know my sheep and my sheep know me." (John 10:14)

- What does the phrase "trust in God" mean to you?

_____

_____

_____

- Is there anything for which trusting in God is unnecessary?

  _____

- Read Philippians 1:8. Did Paul have an undivided heart?

  _____

- Read 2 Corinthians 3:4–5 and Philippians 4:11–13. Would you say that Paul had a steadfast heart and a mind kept in perfect peace?

  _____

  _____

- Read Colossians 1:29. Where was God's energy, His active power, working? From Paul's statement, how is God's energy being expressed on the earth?

  _____

  _____

- Use Paul's life as an example of the relationship between a steadfast heart and trusting in God. Journal your thoughts.

  _____

  _____

Celebration

Worship and celebrate. Contemplate the fact that the glory of God is filling you. He says of you, His dwelling place, ""'I myself will be a wall of fire around it,' declares the LORD, 'and I will be its glory within'"" (Zech. 2:5). Let this thought fill you with wonder.

~ *Day 18* ~

Centering

Begin with centering prayer. Focus your thoughts on the truth of God's presence. In the inner sanctuary of your soul, take a position of worship. Let this be your heart's cry: "Come and see what God has done, / how awesome his works in man's behalf!" (Ps. 66:5).

Meditation

"Since, then, you have been raised with Christ, set your hearts on things above, where Christ is seated at the right hand of God. Set your minds on things above, not on earthly things." (Col. 3:1–2)

A steadfast heart, we have already established, is fixed, steady, immovable. The Word tells us that it is fixed on "things above, where Christ is seated at the right hand of God." In other words, put your mind on the presence of Christ. Don't think of "above" in this verse as a geographical description. Rather it is contrasting the quality of "things above" with "earthly things." The things that flow from Christ are of a better quality and substance than the things that originate in the worldly realm. God uses this same concept in declaring His thoughts higher than our thoughts and His ways higher than our ways (Isa. 55:8–9).

Colossians 3:1–2 reveals that putting our minds on the presence of Christ is, at first, an act of will. "Set" your heart. Place your mind. Fix your thoughts. Do it!

Think of setting your mind—deliberately, intentionally, and willfully focusing your thoughts—as a process similar to setting the dial on your radio receiver. God's living voice is always filling the universe. In fact, His voice contained in the Son's word is what holds the universe together (Heb. 1:3). The question, then, is not, "Is God speaking?" The question is, "Am I hearing?"

In a similar fashion, radio waves are always filling the air. However, the words they carry are not accessible unless the radio waves are picked up by a receiver. God's voice is filling the universe, but His voice only becomes specific and personal to me if I "tune in" to Him spiritually; if I set my mind on things above. The qualities of a radio receiver that are necessary to ensure good reception mirror the qualities of a receptive heart—a heart set on things above.

A receiver with high sensitivity is one that is tuned in to only one frequency. It is highly sensitive to radio waves in that frequency because it is not cluttered with waves from other frequencies. The pray-er who wants to be able to hear God speak must give his or her undivided focus to His living voice. As long as attention is given to worldly frequencies and the voice of the flesh, our sensitivity to God's voice is diminished. If we have set our minds on earthly things, we lose the clarity of God's voice.

Selectivity is the ability of the receiver to obtain signals from one station and reject signals from another station operating on a nearby frequency. Selectivity and high sensitivity go hand-in-hand. Remember that another voice fills the spiritual airwaves—the voice of the deceiver. The pray-er who hears God's voice is the one who recognizes the voice of the father of lies and immediately rejects it.

Do you remember when Peter, with the best of intentions, rebuked Jesus for talking about His impending death? Obviously, the deceiver saw an opportunity to entice Jesus away from His goal by using Peter's mind, which was attuned to worldly frequencies. Wouldn't it seem like the reaction of a good and loving friend to oppose the thought of Jesus' death? But Jesus had selectivity. He knew how to reject Satan's words, no matter what form they took. "Jesus turned and said to Peter, 'Get behind me, Satan! You are a stumbling block to me; you do not have in mind the things of God, but the things of men'" (Matt. 16:23).

Static is a constant problem in receiving radio waves. It is caused by electrical disturbances in the atmosphere. Static distorts sound and often makes words unintelligible. The pray-er who wants to hear God without distortion must remember that "the ruler of the kingdom of the air, the spirit who is now at work in those who are disobedient" (Eph. 2:2) is a reality. The flesh—the part of a believer's nature that is disconnected to the Spirit of God—is the entry point for Satan's noise.

The pray-er who has come to recognize her own flesh-patterns and who continually offers her flesh up for crucifixion when it is exposed will grow her capacity to receive God's voice without interference. The believer who is ignorant of the schemes of the evil one—who does not recognize the flesh when it asserts itself—will be unable to hear God's voice clearly. The freer we are of our flesh, the more attuned we are to the voice of the Father.

God is developing in you a heart that is steadfastly set on Christ. What does that mean? A heart set on things above is not a matter of emulating the life of Jesus as if He were only a historical figure. When you set your mind (heart) on things above, where Christ is seated at the right hand of God, you deliberately focus your mind on the truth of God's Word, which Christ embodies in you, and allow Him to think His thoughts in you. You intentionally put your thought processes, your will, and your feelings at His disposal, allowing Him to make His Word real in your experience as He lives His resurrection life through you.

- Read 2 Corinthians 4:7. Where is God's all-surpassing power?

  _____

  _____

  _____

- Read Ephesians 3:20. Where is God's power at work?

  _____

  _____

  _____

- Read 1 Corinthians 1:24. Who is the power of God?

  _____

  _____

  _____

- If you focus your attention on what is happening in Christ's presence, how will it change your day-to-day living?

  _____

  _____

  _____

Celebration

Worship and celebrate. Contemplate the fact that the glory of God is filling you. He says of you, His dwelling place, ""'I myself will be a wall of fire around it," declares the LORD, "and I will be its glory within"'" (Zech. 2:5). Let this thought fill you with wonder.

~ Day 19 ~

Centering

Begin with centering prayer. Focus your thoughts on the truth of God's presence. In the inner sanctuary of your soul, take a position of worship. Let this be your heart's cry: "Because you are my help, / I sing in the shadow of your wings. / My soul clings to you; / your right hand upholds me" (Ps. 63:7–8).

Meditation

"Everyone who hears these words of mine and puts them into practice is like a wise man who built his house on the rock." (Matt. 7:24)

A steadfast heart is steadfast because it has a solid foundation. How does a heart become steadfast?

In your spiritual life there are two parts: God's giving and your receiving of His gift. This is true in salvation and continues to be true as you live your new life. "Just as you received Christ Jesus as Lord, continue to live in him, rooted and built up in him" (Col. 2:6–7). Your daily spiritual walk works by the same dynamic that brought you eternal salvation. God provides everything and you accept what He provides. God offers everything and you receive what He offers.

Everything that God requires *of you*, He has already provided *for you*. When God provided the ram as the substitute for Isaac (Gen. 22:13–14), He introduced Himself as the "God Who Provides." What does He provide? He provides what He requires. He required a sacrifice and He provided the sacrifice. Remember Abraham's words, "God will provide *for Himself* the lamb" (Gen. 22:8, NASB, italics added). Through the Son's indwelling power, He has already made available everything necessary for living out your new life. "His divine power has given us everything we need for life and godliness through our knowledge of him who called us by his own glory and goodness" (2 Pet. 1:3).

Then comes your part: receiving what He provides. You must make yourself available to all that He has provided. God is very clear about what makes your life available to His power. Obedience. Your obedience opens the way for God to pour His power through you. When you obey, you experience His promises as real and true.

Luke recorded a story from the life of Christ in the seventeenth chapter of his Gospel. Jesus, on His way to Jerusalem, was going into a certain village, and ten lepers met Him and called out to Him for mercy. "When he saw them, he said, 'Go, show yourselves to the priests'" (Luke 17:14). Put yourself in the lepers' place. They didn't know what would unfold. All they knew was that Jesus had told them to go, show themselves to the priests. "And *as they went,* they were cleansed" (Luke 17:14, italics added). Their obedience to the present-tense voice of Jesus released the power and provision of God. God released His power in their obedience.

God made a promise to Joshua. He said, "'I will give you every place *where you set your foot'"* (Josh. 1:3, italics added). As Joshua moved forward, God's power would meet him at every step. So it is with you and with me. As we move forward in response to God's voice, as we live by faith, the power of God will be released in our lives.

We have already seen that God desires a steadfast, undivided heart. We have already seen that He is the One who gives a steadfast heart. How do we receive a steadfast heart? Jesus told a parable to explain how we make ourselves available to what God offers.

"Everyone who hears these words of mine and puts them into practice is like a wise man who built his house on the rock. The rain came down, the streams rose, and the winds blew and beat against that house; yet it did not fall, because it had its foundation on the rock. But everyone who hears these words of mine and does not put them into practice is like a foolish man who built his house on sand. The rain came down, the streams rose, and the winds blew and beat against that house, and it fell with a great crash." (Matt. 7:24–27)

Every act of obedience to the voice of the living and present Jesus steadies the heart. As a house is built brick upon brick, so a steadfast heart is built obedience upon obedience. In big things and small things, with each act of obedience, God is building an undivided heart.

- In Jesus' parable from Matthew 7:24–27, note the words Jesus used to describe each man's circumstances (v. 25 and v. 27). What do you notice?

  _____

  _____

- What point is Jesus making by describing each man's circumstances in exactly the same words?

  _____

  _____

- Will walking in obedience guarantee you easy circumstances? What *does* walking in obedience guarantee?

  _____

  _____

  _____

Celebration

Worship and celebrate. Contemplate the fact that the glory of God is filling you. He says of you, His dwelling place, ""'I myself will be a wall of fire around it,' declares the LORD, 'and I will be its glory within'"" (Zech. 2:5). Let this thought fill you with wonder.

~ Day 20 ~

Review and Reflect

- How would you describe an undivided heart?

_____

_____

_____

- Why is God developing in you an undivided heart?

_____

_____

_____

- How do you see God working in your life right now to wean your heart from other things and fasten it on Him?

_____

_____

_____

- What will be the benefit to you of having an undivided heart?

_____

_____

_____

- What does this verse mean to you?

    Teach me your way, O LORD,
    and I will walk in your truth;
    give me an undivided heart,
    that I may fear your name. (Ps. 86:11)

_____

_____

_____

~ Day 21 ~

Journal Your Thoughts and Prayers

_____

_____

_____

_____

_____

_____

_____

_____

_____

_____

_____

_____

_____

_____

_____

_____

_____

_____

WEEK 4

A Discerning Heart

"Give your servant a discerning heart."
(1 Kings 3:9)

Words that come from the flesh do not have life or power in them. They count for nothing. The discerning heart is filled with the life of Christ and from that Christ-filled repository spills forth His words—words that are spirit and life.

~ *Day* 22 ~

Centering

Begin with centering prayer. Focus on the presence of God that both fills you and surrounds you. Be quiet and let the fact of His powerful presence take deep root in you. Sing to Him, either out loud or in the inner sanctuary of your soul.

Meditation

The heart of the discerning acquires knowledge;
the ears of the wise seek it out. (Prov. 18:15)

God is developing in you a discerning heart. He is crucifying the flesh, flushing out the impurities, and cleaning out the clutter so that He can give you a discerning heart. In 1 Kings 3:9, Solomon asked for a discerning heart. He used a Hebrew word, *shama,* that means "to hear, listen, understand, and obey." Solomon, in asking for a discerning heart, asked for the ability to hear at the deepest level, the level that results in understanding. Jesus once said to His listeners, "'Why is my language not clear to you? Because you are unable to hear what I say'" (John 8:43). It is possible to hear His words but not hear their meaning. A discerning heart understands what the Father says.

As you read Solomon's prayer, your own heart probably identified with it. You were thinking, "That's what I want. I want a hearing heart. I want to discern God's voice." You are responding to God, who has led you to this page in this book on this day, and who is stirring your heart to receive what He offers. Your desire for a hearing heart is the evidence that God is developing one in you.

Because you have submitted to God's work in your heart, because you have started cooperating with Him and His method for cleansing you, the acoustics of your heart are improving daily. The word *acoustics* means "the qualities that determine the ability of an enclosure to reflect sound waves in such a way as to produce distinct hearing." If a structure does not have the proper shape or dimensions, or if it is cluttered with objects that absorb or redirect sound waves, sounds will not be distinct. God is shaping and molding and cleansing your heart so that His voice will be clearly heard. When you can clearly and distinctly hear His voice, you have a discerning heart.

Discernment and spiritual hearing are two parts of a whole. "The heart of the discerning acquires knowledge; / the ears of the wise seek it out" (Prov. 18:15). Persons with discerning hearts—hearts with good acoustics—continually gather knowledge. Everywhere they go, they collect new knowledge. What is their method? Their ears seek it out. They strain their ears for the smallest sound of knowledge. What does knowledge sound like? "The Lord gives wisdom, / and from his mouth come knowledge and understanding" (Prov. 2:6). Knowledge comes only from God's mouth. The discerning heart is always hearing and responding to God's voice.

- Do you feel confident that you can hear God's voice when He speaks in the present? Why or why not?

_____

_____

- Is there anything in your heart that might be limiting its acoustics?

_____

_____

- Are your spiritual ears seeking out God's voice?

_____

_____

_____

Celebration

Celebrate and worship. What are you hearing God say to you right now? Stop and listen. Write it down. Take the time to let it settle in your heart as you relax in His presence.

~ Day 23 ~

Centering

Begin with centering prayer. Focus on the presence of God that both fills you and surrounds you. Be quiet and let the fact of His powerful presence take deep root in you. Sing to Him, either out loud or in the inner sanctuary of your soul.

Meditation

The things that come from the Spirit of God . . .
are spiritually discerned.
(1 Cor. 2:14)

A person who does not have God's Spirit has no hope of understanding spiritual things because all spiritual truth is spiritually discerned. A person who has been born again and so has the Spirit of God, but who is still living according to the flesh will have only the most shallow understanding of spiritual truth. Only the discerning heart can have a clear understanding of God's full truth.

The word *discern* means "to take apart, investigate, look into." The Latin prefix *dis* means "apart" and the word *cernere* means "to sift." The same Latin word yields the words *dissect* and *discriminate.* You can see that the concept of taking something apart is a strong component in *discern.* The Greek word Paul used in 1 Corinthians 2:14 is the word *anakrino.* It means "to inquire into, to sift, to scrutinize." Often it is used in reference to a judicial investigation in which a judge makes careful inquiry into the facts of a case.

The full, rich spiritual truth is not sitting on the surface to be accessed by a casual observer. The deep truths of God for which you are yearning must be spiritually discerned (1 Cor. 2:10). In other words, the deep truths of God are taken apart and investigated in the spirit of a believer under the tutelage of the Spirit of God who dwells in that believer. Then, from the spirit, they are revealed to the understanding. The human intellect on its own cannot investigate the things of the Spirit, neither can it understand them. A person who can discern the things that come from the Spirit of God can also understand the things that come from the Spirit of God. A discerning heart is taught directly by the Lord (Isa. 54:13; John 6:45).

Imagine that I am looking at an X ray. I have no medical training, so even though I am clearly seeing the X ray, I am not understanding it. I do not have the ability to discern what the X ray shows me. I only see it as a whole; I can't mentally take it apart and look into its meaning. I can see it, but it's a mystery to me. Beside me is a doctor. Not only does she see the X ray, but she also discerns the deep truths of the X ray. Therefore, the X ray that is meaningless to me is a source of vital knowledge to her. What is the difference? She has been taught.

The value of a discerning heart is that it can understand and, therefore, live according to spiritual truth. The person who cannot discern spiritual truth is not living in harmony with reality and so is limited in his understanding. "They are darkened in their understanding and separated from the life of God because of the ignorance that is in them due to the hardening of their hearts" (Eph. 4:18).

The illustration Jesus suggested to Nicodemus, that the Spirit is like the wind, may help us understand the value of a discerning heart. The wind has no substance. We don't know where it comes from or where it's going. We can't grab hold of it and feel its texture. We only know about wind because of its effects.

Suppose, then, that a person decides that he does not believe in the wind. Wind, he decides, is the figment of someone's imagination. No one can prove wind. He prefers to stick to things that can be empirically proven. This person will reach some distorted conclusions about what is true. He will have a skewed view of reality. For example, this person may conclude that trees lean over all by themselves sometimes; or that leaves lying quietly on the ground sometimes jump up and twirl through the air. He will not understand that the trees and the leaves are responding to a power that is acting upon them.

If a person who does not believe in the wind and a person who believes in and understands the wind look at the same scene, they will see two startlingly different "truths." The first will see trees bending over; the second will see the wind.

The person who learns to observe with spirit-eyes will look at earth and see the Spirit. He or she will know and understand the whole truth of spiritual reality and will not be limited to time-bound, earth-bound perceptions and short-sighted vision. Seeing the truth, he or she will be free to live in harmony with it, no longer bound to, or limited by, a caricature of the truth. Jesus said, "'If you hold to my teaching, you are really my disciples. Then you will know the truth, and *the truth will set you free*'" (John 8:31, italics added).[17]

The discerning heart has been taught by the Lord, and when it comes in contact with spiritual truth, it receives knowledge. What was once hidden, or a mystery, the Spirit reveals to the discerning heart (Rom. 16:25; 1 Cor. 2:7; Eph. 3:9; Col. 1:26).

- When you look at the circumstances facing you, are you taking into account spiritual truth? Or are you seeing only surface truth? Explain.

  _____

  _____

- Will you ask the Father to give you discernment? Write out your specific requests.

  _____

  _____

  _____

Celebration

Celebrate and worship. What are you hearing God say to you right now? Stop and listen. Write it down. Take the time to let it settle in your heart as you relax in His presence.

_____

Centering

Begin with centering prayer. Focus on the presence of God that both fills you and surrounds you. Be quiet and let the fact of His powerful presence take deep root in you. Sing to Him, either out loud or in the inner sanctuary of your soul.

Meditation

I am your servant; give me discernment
that I may understand your statutes. (Ps. 119:125)

Understanding is the goal of discernment. God wants you to understand Him, His ways, and His Word.

- Read 1 Corinthians 2:12. Why have we received the Spirit of God?

  _____

- Define the word *understand.* Use a dictionary or describe your own sense of the word.

  _____

  _____

- Does understanding differ from knowledge? In what way? Can you know something but not understand it?

  _____

  _____

  _____

Understanding takes knowledge one step further. For example, I may know a mathematical equation such as πr^2 because I have memorized it. I may know how to say it; I may know how to write it; I may know how to use it to answer the question, "How do you find the area of a circle?" But I still may not understand it. I may know it and yet it still has no meaning to me.

A discerning heart can turn knowledge into understanding, because it is the dwelling place for the Spirit of God who understands the deep things of God (1 Cor. 2:10). Remember that to discern means to take apart and to sift. In your spirit-center, you take apart the truths of God and look into their mystery. Then you put them back together into a form that your intellect can recognize and assign meaning to. You know their inner workings.

Compare this process with the way your physical brain reaches understanding from the stimuli it receives from your environment. When, for example, your eyes see an object, signals are sent to the visual cortex, where layers of cells complete specialized functions. Some sense colors. Some sense shapes. Some sense depth. Some are so specialized that they detect two lines that connect to form an angle and nothing else. It's as if the visual cortex consisted of billions of highly trained, exquisitely specialized observers, each responsible for one thing and one thing only, no matter what the overall scene being viewed. Put all these specialized mini-pictures together and you have a splendidly detailed, beautifully colored picture. The incoming information is processed and refined so that all the data about the object being viewed—its size, distance, shape, color, location, and relationship to the background—is assembled into one coherent image. Then this information is sent to another part of the brain, the hippocampus or the memory storage area, where the new information is checked against the stored data. Then, in a matter of milliseconds, the information is transmitted to other brain areas where its meaning is translated and decisions are made as to what, if any, action should be taken in response to it. Amazing, isn't it? Doesn't that make you want to burst out in praise to such a Creator? "I praise you because I am fearfully and wonderfully made; / your works are wonderful, / I know that full well" (Ps. 139:14).

The amazing way that God created your brain is only an inadequate picture of how your spirit-center, infused with the Spirit of the living God, turns spiritual knowledge into understanding. When you respond from your spirit-center, not from your flesh, to the Word of God and the truths of the spiritual realm, your spirit dissects that information, sifts it, looks into it; your spirit-center turns it upside down and inside out and then puts it all back together into a form that your intellect recognizes. The discerning heart has an understanding of the things of God. What happens when we understand the things of God? "Give me understanding, and I will keep your law / and obey it with all my heart" (Ps. 119:34). When I understand a law, I naturally obey it. For example, I do not jump off of cliffs, because I understand the law of gravity. As God gives you deep understanding, obedience becomes your natural reaction. You will understand when He teaches you. "I have not departed from your laws, / for you yourself have taught me. . . . / I gain understanding from your precepts; / therefore I hate every wrong path" (Ps. 119:102–104).

- At what point are you finding it difficult to obey what you know God is telling you? Do you believe that it is because, at a deep level, you do not understand it? If so, will you ask God to give you discernment so that you can understand? Write out your thoughts.

_____

_____

_____

Celebration

Celebrate and worship. What are you hearing God say to you right now? Stop and listen. Write it down. Take the time to let it settle in your heart as you relax in His presence.

~ Day 25 ~

Centering

Begin with centering prayer. Focus on the presence of God that both fills you and surrounds you. Be quiet and let the fact of His powerful presence take deep root in you. Sing to Him, either out loud or in the inner sanctuary of your soul.

Meditation

Show me your ways, O Lord,
teach me your paths. (Ps. 25:4)

The ability to discern truth is a result of the active and present work of the Spirit in your heart. He is creating a discerning heart in you as He lives in you and has more and more access to your thoughts, your time, and your heart. His discernment, given to you, brings understanding. He and He alone knows the heart and mind of the Father and the Son. He is teaching you, guiding you into truth. When He teaches you, knowledge becomes understanding and then you have a discerning heart.

The cry of a discerning heart is, "Show me your ways, O Lord; / teach me your paths" (Ps. 25:4). *Show* me your ways.

Cooking is not a skill that comes naturally to me. However, I have a friend who seems to put together wonderful meals without effort. From time to time, I call on her expertise. "Libby, tell me how you make that delicious casserole," I plead. Libby begins to describe exactly how to make the casserole, but she instructs with words like *mince* and *sauté* and other terms that are outside my vocabulary. Finally she abandons verbal explanation: "Come over. I'll *show* you how to make it."

Show me your ways, O Lord! He does not teach on an academic, arms-length plain. He enters into your "now." He engages you in the first person. He fully invests Himself in your experience and causes you to understand.

When you understand any spiritual truth, it is because the process of discernment has occurred in your spirit. When that truth begins to transform your life—your actions and your thought processes—then discernment has created understanding.

> Who is wise? He will realize these things.
>   Who is discerning? He will understand them.
> The ways of the LORD are right;
>   the righteous walk in them,
>   but the rebellious stumble in them. (Hos. 14:9)

- Spend time with this prayer: "Show me your ways, O LORD; / teach me your paths" (Ps. 25:4). Let the Spirit elaborate on these thoughts. Turn them into petition for your specific circumstances. Write out your prayer.

_____

_____

_____

Celebration

Celebrate and worship. What are you hearing God say to you right now? Stop and listen. Write it down. Take the time to let it settle in your heart as you relax in His presence.

_____

~ Day 26 ~

Centering

Begin with centering prayer. Focus on the presence of God that both fills you and surrounds you. Be quiet and let the fact of His powerful presence take deep root in you. Sing to Him, either out loud or in the inner sanctuary of your soul.

Meditation

Wisdom is found on the lips of the discerning. (Prov. 10:13)

Once you have a discerning heart so that your mind is filled with understanding of the deep truths of God, that understanding begins to flow from your mouth as water flows from a fountain. "The mouth of the righteous . . . is a fountain of life," and "The mouth of the righteous brings forth wisdom" (Prov. 10:11, 31). The heart is the wellspring of life, the source from which all else flows (Prov. 4:23). Words of life flow out of a discerning heart.

Jesus said that words reveal the inner being. "'The good man brings good things out of the good stored up in his heart, and the evil man brings evil things out of the evil stored up in his heart. For out of the overflow of his heart his mouth speaks'" (Luke 6:45). If your heart, or mind, is filled with the fruit of discernment—understanding generated by the Spirit— then you begin to speak truth taught by the Spirit. These words, because they were originated in the Spirit, are spiritual words. They convey spiritual truth and carry spiritual power (John 3:6; 1 Cor. 2:13). Jesus said of His words, "'The Spirit gives life; the flesh counts for nothing. The words I have spoken to you are spirit and they are life'" (John 6:63). Only Jesus has the words that are life (John 6:68). Jesus' words are spirit and life because the Spirit gives life to them. The Spirit breathes into them the breath of life. Words that come from the flesh do not have life or power in them. They count for nothing. The discerning heart is filled with the life of Christ and from that Christ-filled repository spills forth His words—words that are spirit and life.

The person with a discerning heart will find herself speaking words that are uplifting, instructive, encouraging, and life-giving. She knows "the word that sustains the weary" (Isa. 50:4). She will not have to struggle and strive to come up with these life-filled words; they will be the natural fruit of her discerning heart. "A wise man's heart guides his mouth, / and his lips promote instruction" (Prov. 16:23).

- Read Luke 6:43–45. According to this parable, how did Jesus relate "tree and fruit" to "heart and words"?

  _____

  _____

- Read Proverbs 12:18, 15:4, 18:21, and James 3:5–8. Summarize what the Word of God says about the power of words in the lives of others.

  _____

  _____

- Read Hebrews 11:3. How was the universe created?

  _____

  _____

- Read Hebrews 4:12 and Isaiah 55:11. Summarize what the Word of God says about the power of God's words.

  _____

  _____

  _____

- Read Isaiah 51:16, 59:21, Jeremiah 1:9, and Romans 10:8. What do you think God means by saying His words will be in your mouth? Look at Matthew 10:19–20 and Luke 12:11–12 for clarification.

_____

_____

_____

Celebration

Celebrate and worship. What are you hearing God say to you right now? Stop and listen. Write it down. Take the time to let it settle in your heart as you relax in His presence.

_____

Review and Reflect

- What is a discerning heart?

_____

_____

- Why is a discerning heart necessary?

_____

_____

- How does your flesh interfere with discernment?

_____

_____

- How do you see God working in your life right now to develop discernment in you?

_____

_____

- What do you need to do to cooperate with Him?

_____

_____

- What does this verse mean to you?
  The heart of the discerning acquires knowledge;
  the ears of the wise seek it out. (Prov. 18:15)

_____

_____

~ Day 28 ~

Journal Your Thoughts and Prayers

_____

_____

_____

_____

_____

_____

_____

_____

_____

_____

_____

_____

_____

_____

_____

_____

_____

_____

_____

WEEK 5

A Rejoicing Heart

Glory in his holy name;
let the hearts of those who seek the LORD rejoice.
(1 Chron. 16:10)

The joy that flows from Jesus into your heart is outside of and beyond circumstances. It is a joy that surpasses the happiness that earthly success brings. True joy is so Christ-centered that earthly success can neither add to it nor diminish it.

~ Day 29 ~

Centering

Begin with centering prayer. Let your mind rest in the powerful presence of the Father. Let the supernatural peace that radiates from Him saturate your soul. Let Him so fill you with thoughts of Himself that no room is left for anxiety.

Meditation

But may all who seek you
rejoice and be glad in you;
may those who love your salvation always say,
"Let God be exalted!" (Ps. 70:4)

Joy marks the life of the person whose heart belongs exclusively to the Father. Joy is impossible to define in words. It can be known only by experiencing it. Joy is an emotion that comes out of your spirit-center. The flesh has a shadow-version of joy called "happiness" or "pleasure." But the flesh's version is flat, one-dimensional, and transitory. Unlike happiness, which comes and goes with circumstances, joy's core is spiritual. Joy is continually in effect because it is based on the solid and unchanging nature of God.

The joy that Spirit-led Christians experience is the very joy of the indwelling Christ being expressed through their souls. Jesus prayed for His disciples "'so that they may have the full measure of my joy within them'" (John 17:13). Restated with the nuances of the Greek, "Father, let My followers be filled to the brim and overflowing with the joy that I possess. I will be in them pouring My own joy into their hearts."

The heart that has passed through crucifixion and is continually sloughing away flesh is able to receive the river of joy flowing through it.

When you and I experience joy, it is His joy we experience. Joy has no other source. "All my springs *of joy* are in you" (Ps. 87:7, NASB).

Joy, because it is based in eternal truth instead of momentary events, is always available to the believer, no matter what circumstance arises. The flesh blocks the flow of joy, causing the heart to be resistant to joy. The flesh focuses on the situation as it appears from an earthly perspective, and the flesh attributes power to circumstances. The flesh's earth-bound perspective interrupts the flow of joy. However, the Spirit-saturated soul is filled with joy in every circumstance. Your spirit-center transfused with His life can look at every circumstance in the light of His presence. In that light, you are able to see circumstances from a new perspective. Factors once hidden in shadow are exposed. More of the full picture is in view. And it is framed in the goodness and the sovereignty of God.

> Child, I know all about the situation that is worrying you right now. I knew about it before you did. Believe me when I tell you it is finished. Your prayers are bringing the finished work out of the spiritual realm to establish it in the material realm. You do not see the finished work in the earth environment yet, but earth is not your home. Do you know why you are having difficulty believing right now? Because you have only looked at the situation in the artificial light of the earth kingdom. Earth kingdom's light only shows up the need. Bring it to Me. Spend time with Me in your true kingdom. Look at it in the Eternal Light. I will blot out the need and illumine only the supply. Come![18]

If you could see His whole plan from beginning to end, see His purposes and His heart, see how this very circumstance was being used for long-term profit, then you would choose to be right where you are. It all comes down to this one thing: *Him.* You can be filled with uninterrupted joy because of who He is. "May all who seek you / rejoice and be glad in you; / may those who love your salvation always say, / 'Let God be exalted!'" (Ps. 70:4).

- What circumstances in your life have you viewed only in the artificial light of earth?

_____

_____

_____

- View them now from your place in His presence. Describe the difference.

_____

_____

_____

Celebration

Offer Him your difficult circumstances as avenues through which He may display His power. Let your surrender be an act of worship, in spirit and in truth. The Father is seeking such worshipers. Rejoice!

~ Day 30 ~

Centering

Begin with centering prayer. Let your mind rest in the powerful presence of the Father. Let the supernatural peace that radiates from Him saturate your soul. Let Him so fill you with thoughts of Himself that no room is left for anxiety.

Meditation

"I have told you this so that my joy may be in you and that your joy may be complete." (John 15:11)

Jesus was filled with joy. We are mistaken to think that, in His earthly visage, He was somber and melancholy. Scripture paints Him as witty and outgoing and charismatic and winsome. Children loved to be with Him. He was invited to parties. In fact, His enemies criticized Him for having too much fun. "'For John the Baptist came neither eating bread nor drinking wine, and you say, "He has a demon." The Son of Man came eating and drinking, and you say, "Here is a glutton and a drunkard, a friend of tax collectors and 'sinners'"'" (Luke 7:33–34). Jesus also showed us that the Father is filled with joy.

That joyful Jesus lives in you and in me. His plan is that you will be the conduit through which He expresses His joy. He wants His joy to be in you, and He wants your joy to be complete. The Greek word translated *complete* means to be filled to the brim so that nothing is lacking. He wants you to have the fullness of His joy.

"'I have told you this *so that* my joy may be in you and that your joy may be complete'" (John 15:11, italics added). What will result from being filled with His joy?

- Read John 15:1–11. How does Jesus describe the relationship between Himself and His disciples?

  _____

  _____

  _____

- What is the life that flows through the branch?

  _____

  _____

  _____

- Does the branch have any life flowing through it other than the vine's life?

  _____

  _____

  _____

- Does the branch have *any* life of its own?

  _____

  _____

  _____

- Sum up what Jesus said about how His joy is made available to His disciples.

_____

_____

_____

Jesus wants to pour His joy into you. His joy is based on His knowledge of the Father. He knows that the Father is always working according to an eternal plan, a plan that has a good, productive, and beneficial outcome. He knows that nothing occurs outside of the Father's sovereignty and that He can always rejoice in what the Father is bringing about. He endured the cross and its shame by keeping His eyes on the outcome: the joy that was set before Him (Heb. 12:2).

When His life flows through you, His faith flows through you, His joy flows through you, and His strength flows through you. What is facing you right now? Do you think that Jesus is worried or anxious about it? Or do you think that Jesus is absolutely certain that this circumstance is positioning you and preparing you for the fullness of the Spirit and for the next step in the Father's plan? Yield yourself to His life within you. Let Him fill you full of His joy even in the midst of challenging circumstances.

Celebration

Offer Him your difficult circumstances as avenues through which He may display His power. Let your surrender be an act of worship, in spirit and in truth. The Father is seeking such worshipers. Rejoice!

~ Day 31 ~

Centering

Begin with centering prayer. Let your mind rest in the powerful presence of the Father. Let the supernatural peace that radiates from Him saturate your soul. Let Him so fill you with thoughts of Himself that no room is left for anxiety.

Meditation

You have filled my heart with greater joy
than when their grain and new wine abound. (Ps. 4:7)

The joy that flows from Jesus into your heart is outside of and beyond circumstances. It is a joy that surpasses the happiness that earthly success brings. True joy is so Christ-centered that earthly success can neither add to it nor diminish it.

Success in the earthly realm is not wrong. In fact, it is a gift from God He wants you to enjoy with Him. In the old covenant, God established the Feast of Tabernacles as a seven-day celebration of the harvest. His instructions were: "For seven days celebrate the Feast to the LORD your God at the place the LORD will choose. For the LORD your God will bless you in all your harvest and in all the work of your hands, and your joy will be complete" (Deut. 16:15). God wants you to take great pleasure in what He provides and to find joy in it because you know it came from Him.

However, there will be other times when His blessings and His favor do not come in material, financial, or other physical forms. There will be times when, from an earthly point of view, it appears that God is withholding His blessing. There will be times when your circumstances don't seem to be the platform for God's power. Then what?

Though the fig tree does not bud
   and there are no grapes on the vines,
though the olive crop fails
   and the fields produce no food,
though there are no sheep in the pen
   and no cattle in the stalls,
yet I will rejoice in the LORD,
   I will be joyful in God my Savior. (Hab. 3:17–18)

Joy, when it is truly joy, will not abandon you even then. Under the surface of your emotions you will discover a strong undercurrent of joy. It is His joy. It is eternal; it is changeless; it is His gift to you.

You can rejoice because you know that God is in control. You can rejoice because you know that God is working everything out for His good purposes. You can rejoice in advance for what God will do. You can rejoice because you know that nothing is too difficult for Him and nothing is impossible for Him. You can rejoice because He is doing something that is beyond what you can ask or even imagine. You can rejoice *in the Lord.*

- What circumstances in your life are not working out, or didn't work out, as you thought God would work them out?

  _____

  _____

  _____

- What do your emotions tell you about your situations? Upon what are those emotions based?

  _____

  _____

- Invite the indwelling Jesus to fill you with His joy, based on truth. Write out your invitation.

_____

_____

_____

Celebration

Offer Him your difficult circumstances as avenues through which He may display His power. Let your surrender be an act of worship, in spirit and in truth. The Father is seeking such worshipers. Rejoice!

~ Day 32 ~

Centering

Begin with centering prayer. Let your mind rest in the powerful presence of the Father. Let the supernatural peace that radiates from Him saturate your soul. Let Him so fill you with thoughts of Himself that no room is left for anxiety.

Meditation

My soul will be satisfied as with the richest of foods;
with singing lips my mouth will praise you. (Ps. 63:5)

Joy expresses itself in praise. Praise is the spontaneous and natural outflow of the inflow of His life. When my soul is satisfied as if it had feasted on the richest of foods, when my soul is flooded with His life, then praise spills over.

C. S. Lewis, in his *Reflections on the Psalms,* observed the experience of praise. He began to notice that people spontaneously praise whatever they value and spontaneously urge others to join them in praising it. "I think we delight to praise what we enjoy because the praise not merely expresses but completes the enjoyment; it is its appointed consummation. It is not out of compliment that lovers keep on telling one another how beautiful they are; the delight is incomplete till it is expressed. It is frustrating to have discovered a new author and not to be able to tell anyone how good he is; or to come suddenly, at the turn of the road, upon some mountain valley of unexpected grandeur and then to have to keep silent because the people with you care for it no more than for a tin can in the ditch; to hear a good joke and find no one to share it with."[19]

Praise completes the experience of joy. The more my soul is filled with Him, the more of His joy that floods me, the more "my mouth is filled with [His] praise" (Ps. 71:8) and "my lips overflow with praise" (Ps. 119:171).

The key to true joy, we've seen, is that it is joy in the Lord. The key to authentic praise is that it expresses a satisfied soul. The soul can only be satisfied with the presence of God through the indwelling life of Christ because that is its design. Because God has "set eternity in the hearts of men" (Eccles. 3:11), nothing less than eternity—nothing temporal—will satisfy. God says, "'I will fill the soul of the priests with abundance, / And My people shall be satisfied with My goodness'" (Jer. 31:14, NASB). The word translated *fill* means to saturate. He will saturate our souls (we are priests according to 1 Pet. 2:5, 9) with His abundance, and it will satisfy us. His abundance will satiate that soul-craving that is born in us. And when our souls are satisfied as if they had dined on the richest food, praise will instinctively flow.

Not only will praise complete the experience of joy, but it will also multiply the joy. In the times when your emotions are at their lowest and when the joy of the Lord seems faint, begin to offer praise. Your freewill offering of praise will put your flesh on the cross because praise is the deathblow to self-life. Your decision to offer praise will give the Spirit ascendancy over your flesh. Praise is one of the most powerful weapons in your war against the flesh-life.

As you genuinely praise God, basing your praise on truth—though it begins as a deliberate act on your part—it is very likely to transform into praise that engages your emotions and opens them to Jesus' joy. Again, joy is a work of the Spirit; its indestructibility will astound you.

- Write out a psalm of praise to the Lord, making it specific to your circumstances.

_____

_____

_____

_____

Celebration

Offer Him your difficult circumstances as avenues through which He may display His power. Let your surrender be an act of worship, in spirit and in truth. The Father is seeking such worshipers. Rejoice!

~ Day 33 ~

Centering

Begin with centering prayer. Let your mind rest in the powerful presence of the Father. Let the supernatural peace that radiates from Him saturate your soul. Let Him so fill you with thoughts of Himself that no room is left for anxiety.

Meditation

Sing joyfully to the LORD, you righteous;
it is fitting for the upright to praise him. (Ps. 33:1)

Praise fits you. And praise fits God. Praise is fitting—appropriate, right, suitable.

As you praise, you are releasing tremendous spiritual power. Praise dispels the enemy's troops. Praise lays the groundwork for the display of God's power. "He who sacrifices thank offerings honors me, / and he prepares the way / so that I may show him the salvation of God" (Ps. 50:23).

God inhabits the praises of His people (Ps. 22:3, KJV). I struggled with this concept for a long time, because it seemed to mean that my praise created or enticed God's presence. That idea is inconsistent with the whole counsel of God. Instead, I think it implies that the praises of His people have God's life in them. In the spiritual realm, God is always the initiator and the giver and we are always the responders and the receivers. This is true even in praise. The Spirit of the Son in us stirs up praise and brings to our thoughts all the reasons God is worthy of our praise. God expresses His joy through our praise. When I praise God it is really the Son praising through me. I speak the words of praise that He speaks in me. His words coming out of my mouth have the life of God in them, because He has the words of life. The praises of God's people have God's life in them; He inhabits the praises of His people.

Praise fits you. You were created "for the praise of his glory" (Eph. 1:12). So your soul, praising Him, fulfills the purpose for which it was designed. Praising is fitting.

Praise fits God. "Great is the LORD and most worthy of praise; / his greatness no one can fathom" (Ps. 145:3). He is worthy of praise. You have, I'm sure, been around a person who needed an inordinate amount of praise and who sought it constantly. This uncomfortable situation becomes wearying. Perhaps you've also received praise far beyond what was necessary or deserved. This too was an uncomfortable situation. In these cases, the praise was not fitting. The object of praise was not worthy. Only God is worthy. Praising God, who is worthy to be praised, is invigorating instead of wearying, because it is fitting.

Praise releases faith. As you praise God, keeping the eyes of your heart focused on Him, you find that faith is present in you. Praise keeps you centered on Him. It keeps your attention on the supply rather than the need. When your attention is fixed on Him, problems, needs, and circumstances all take their proper perspective.

I want you to do an experiment. Stare fixedly at an object for several seconds. Do you notice that the peripheral objects become unfocused and only your object of fixation is sharply focused? This is a picture of truth in the spiritual realm. If you fixate on the problem, it will grow to gigantic proportions. If, however, you fixate on the Father, He will be magnified in your heart and faith will grow strong. Magnify the Lord through praise. Paul wrote, "So we fix our eyes not on what is seen, but on what is unseen. For what is seen is temporary, but what is unseen is eternal" (2 Cor. 4:18). Praise fixes our eyes on what is unseen.

- Take time to consciously allow the Spirit of the Son in you to stir up praise. Be aware of this spiritual dynamic. Spend an extended time in praise. Write it; speak it; sing it.

_____

_____

• As you read these thoughts on praise, what specific message did the Spirit speak to you? What truth grabbed hold of your heart and settled in?

_____

_____

_____

Celebration

Offer Him your difficult circumstances as avenues through which He may display His power. Let your surrender be an act of worship, in spirit and in truth. The Father is seeking such worshipers. Rejoice!

~ Day 34 ~

Review and Reflect

- How does joy differ from happiness or pleasure?

  _____

  _____

- How do you see the supernatural joy of Jesus being expressed in your life?

  _____

  _____

- Write down some specific grounds for praise in the midst of your most difficult circumstance.

  _____

  _____

- Why must you be increasing in your understanding and knowledge of God for praise to be genuine?

  _____

  _____

- What does this verse mean to you?

      But as for me, I will always have hope;
      I will praise you more and more. (Ps. 71:14)

  _____

  _____

Journal Your Thoughts and Prayers

_____

_____

_____

_____

_____

_____

_____

_____

_____

_____

_____

_____

_____

_____

_____

_____

_____

_____

_____

_____

_____

WEEK 6

An Overflowing Heart

*"If anyone is thirsty, let him come to me and drink.
Whoever believes in me, as the Scripture has said,
streams of living water will flow from within him."*
(John 7:37–38)

Out of our brokenness comes the powerful overflow of
His life—the God of all comfort comforts others
through us. . . . The very comfort we have received
becomes the comfort with which we minister to others.
What He has poured into us, He also pours out through
us to those in our world.

~ Day 36 ~

Centering

Begin with centering prayer. In the inner sanctuary of your soul, stand before the Father with your arms outstretched and your hands lifted to Him. Ask Him to fill your soul with His abundance. Open your life to His power and provision. Don't rush—speak to Him about your openness and listen for His word to you.

Meditation

"If a man remains in me and I in him, he will bear much fruit; apart from me you can do nothing." (John 15:5)

The life of the vine flowing through the branches produces the vine's fruit. The branch displays the fruit. The fruit that is produced on the branch is the proof of the vine's life.

Jesus explained that His life flowing through His people will produce His fruit.

In John 15:1–8 Jesus gives a graphic teaching about His indwelling life. The picture of the vine and the branches illustrates the truth that He will live through believers. The language He used in this passage—the branch remaining in the vine—suggests that the branch was grafted into the vine. In the grafting process, the heart of the vine and the heart of the branch must both be exposed. Heart must be grafted to heart. If the grafting is successful, the heart of the vine becomes the heart of the branch. The branch has been cut off from its old life and grafted into its new life. It has died to the old vine and has become alive to the new vine. Only then can new life flow.

You have been cut off from your life of flesh and grafted into His heart. Entirely new life flows through you—eternal life. The life that flows through you is self-giving love. The life with which He longs to flood you is a life of aggressive, seeking, saving love. This life will offend your flesh; it will disrupt your flesh; it will expose your flesh. The love that flows through you is a lay-down-your-life kind of love. It's a die-to-your-flesh kind of love. But, above all, it's a love filled with the power of God to save and heal and lift up.

We are the dispensers of His life. What He wants to do in your world, He will do through you. His life in you will call on you to lay aside fleshly agendas and fleshly methods. It will require you to have your spiritual senses on full alert at all times so that your love will be directed by Him. You will have to flow in His spirit because there will be no rule book or formula, only His present-tense power to guide you. You will never have to ask, "What would Jesus do?" You will ask, "Jesus, what are You doing? And what do You want to do through me?"

The Father will put you where He wants you. He will bring into your life or to your attention everyone He wants to love through you. You've already been assigned. "For we are God's workmanship, created in Christ Jesus to do good works, which God prepared in advance for us to do" (Eph. 2:10). You will not have to find God's will; God's will finds you.

When His life flows through you to others, you will have the privilege of seeing the power of God at work. It will produce in you exuberant joy. The secret is to be ministering out of the Spirit, not from the flesh. The flesh produces the form of godliness without the power (2 Tim. 3:5).

A person can act in servant ways without having a servant heart. Many times servant actions are actually ways to manipulate people and win their favor. Other times servant actions come from a sense of inferiority or even guilt. Often, others can't tell the difference between the servant actions that come from the flesh and the servant actions that come from the Spirit of God in you. In fact, sometimes we can't tell ourselves. Only the Word of God can divide between soul and spirit (Heb. 4:12). Because the Word of God is "living and active" (which means that it is powerful, it has life in it, it is producing effect, and it has energy), it can separate flesh-based motivations and actions from Spirit-breathed motivations and actions. Let the Word of God work in you to flay the flesh from your motivations and leave only "his energy, which so powerfully works in [you]" (Col. 1:29).

Let His love flowing through you continue to flush out the pockets of flesh it finds. Let the Spirit of Him who raised Christ Jesus from the dead give life to your mortal body (Rom. 8:11). Let that life flow through you to those around you.

- What situation is in your life right now where God is calling on you to love with His supernatural love?

  _____

  _____

  _____

- Is your flesh resisting?

  _____

  _____

  _____

- Will you choose to set aside your flesh-life? Write out your thoughts.

  _____

  _____

  _____

Celebration

Celebrate and worship. Looking to the Spirit for guidance, take time to give careful thought to the enormity of the Father's love for you. Think about His love concretely and tangibly. Celebrate His love.

~ *Day 37* ~

Centering

Begin with centering prayer. In the inner sanctuary of your soul, stand before the Father with your arms outstretched and your hands lifted to Him. Ask Him to fill your soul with His abundance. Open your life to His power and provision. Don't rush—speak to Him about your openness and listen for His word to you.

Meditation

When I am weak, then I am strong. (2 Cor. 12:10)

The person who has learned to let the death of Jesus always be in operation has discovered this dichotomy: my strength is my weakness and my weakness is my strength.

All of us have natural strengths. We quickly learn to depend on those strengths to get what we want. We learn how to use those strengths to our best advantage. Once we begin to surrender our flesh to crucifixion, the first thing to die must be the strength of our flesh. "No," you might be saying. "God will use my strengths for His glory. After all, He gave them to me, didn't He?" My friend, nothing in your flesh is of any use to God. Your flesh must be broken and crucified.

Moses was a man who was naturally gifted and skilled and trained. In the book of Acts we read, "Moses was educated in all the wisdom of the Egyptians and was powerful in speech and action" (Acts 7:22). We know from extrabiblical sources that Moses was a leader in Egypt and successful in many areas. Moses was chosen by the pharaoh, who had no son of his own, to be his successor. Moses had everything going for him.

Moses was God's handpicked choice to lead His people out of bondage. At forty years old, at the height of his power, Moses apparently felt and embraced God's call. In fact, you might imagine that Moses thought,

"What a fine choice God has made. I am certainly in a position to lead the Israelites and I definitely have the ability." Scripture gives us a glimpse into Moses' self-confidence: "Moses thought that his own people would realize that God was using him to rescue them, but they did not" (v. 25). God then exiled Moses to the desert for forty years. Do you see the problem? Moses' strength was in God's way.

We have only sketchy details about Moses' desert years, but enough to know that he went from being among the most admired men in Egypt to being an unknown shepherd for someone else's sheep. When God had finished training Moses in the desert, He appeared to Moses in a burning bush. What a changed man Moses was! Remember that forty years before, in the strength of his flesh, he had assumed that anyone could see that he was being used by God to rescue Israel. This time an altogether different Moses said, "'Who am I, that I should go to Pharaoh and bring the Israelites out of Egypt?'" (Exod. 3:11). Brokenness characterized Moses, strength revealed as weakness. Moses was emptied of flesh and was ready to be filled with the power of God.

Because strength was revealed as weakness, weakness could be revealed as strength. God's strength and power are brought to full measure, or "made perfect," where the strength of flesh has been broken (2 Cor. 12:8). Paul put it this way: "When I am weak, then I am strong" (2 Cor. 12:10). In other words, "When my Paul-flesh is crucified then Jesus-life flows." What does God want from you? He wants your weakness. He wants your brokenness.

Like Moses, Jacob was a man with great natural strength. He was skillful at molding circumstances and manipulating events to bring about the outcome he desired. He trusted in the strength of his flesh. God intended to use Jacob to fulfill His plan (Gen. 28:13–14), but Jacob's flesh-strength had to be broken before the power of God could be put on display in him. The defining moment—the crucifixion moment—came at a place Jacob named Peniel.

Jacob, having sent his family and his servants ahead, was alone. God came to Jacob in the form of "a man" and wrestled with him all night long. I want you to notice that God approached Jacob and initiated this wrestling match. The goal of a wrestling match is to have your opponent flat on the ground and helpless. Jacob resisted God and would not surrender, so greatly did he value his flesh-strength. But God, determined to bring Jacob to the place of victory, reached out and "touched the socket of Jacob's hip so that his hip was wrenched as he wrestled" (Gen. 32:25).

The hip joint is the strongest joint in the human body. The thigh muscle is the strongest muscle in the human body. God broke Jacob at the point of his greatest strength. The wrestling match was over. Jacob, now broken and helpless, said to God, "'I will not let you go unless you bless me'" (v. 26) Jacob at his strongest could not have held God captive. Certainly in his brokenness he could not. Yet the Scripture seems to imply that God could not leave Jacob. Do you know why I think it was? It was not that God did not have the strength to break Jacob's grip; it is that He did not have the heart to break Jacob's grip. When in his brokenness and helplessness Jacob clung to God and cried out to Him from the depths of his own weakness, God declared Jacob a winner. "'Your name will no longer be Jacob, but Israel, because you have struggled with God and with men and have overcome'" (v. 28). When did God say Jacob had won? When he lost.

When He has your weakness, He can let His life flow through you to those around you. He can demonstrate His love and His power as He lives and acts through you. You will be like Paul: "Therefore I will boast all the more gladly about my weaknesses, so that Christ's power may rest on me" (2 Cor. 12:9).

- What are the strengths of your flesh?

  _____

  _____

- How has God taken you through circumstances to reveal your strengths as weaknesses? Is He doing that right now?

  _____

  _____

- Will you admit your strength to be weakness and invite His power to rest on you? Write out your thoughts and/or prayer.

_____

_____

_____

Celebration

Celebrate and worship. Looking to the Spirit for guidance, take time to give careful thought to the enormity of the Father's love for you. Think about His love concretely and tangibly. Celebrate His love.

~ Day 38 ~

Centering

Begin with centering prayer. In the inner sanctuary of your soul, stand before the Father with your arms outstretched and your hands lifted to Him. Ask Him to fill your soul with His abundance. Open your life to His power and provision. Don't rush—speak to Him about your openness and listen for His word to you.

Meditation

We can comfort those in any trouble with the comfort
we ourselves have received from God. (2 Cor. 1:4)

Out of our brokenness comes the powerful overflow of His life—the God of all comfort comforts others through us (2 Cor. 1:3–7). The very comfort we have received becomes the comfort with which we minister to others. What He has poured into us, He also pours out through us to those in our world.

We have seen that Jesus' physical crucifixion is the death into which we enter. And His resurrection is the resurrection that is manifested in us. When Jesus was physically resurrected, all that was from earth—the limiting, earth-bound body He lived in for a time—was left behind. Resurrection separated eternal from temporal. The body of His resurrection was perfect and eternal. It is the very body in which He ascended from earth to take His place at the right hand of the Father. This perfect, resurrected body retained its scars.

How often our pride, or our mistaken sense that we need to present a perfect front to those in our care, causes us to think of our wounds and our scars as something to hide; something ugly; something demeaning; something that lessens our value. But look at Jesus. Look at what Jesus thought of His wounds: "Here, Thomas. Look at My wounds. Touch My scars.

These are the proof of My resurrection. I bear the marks of death, but I am alive!" Jesus knew His wounds were beautiful.

Thomas said, "'Unless I see the nail marks in his hands and put my finger where the nails were, and put my hand into his side, I will not believe it'" (John 20:25). My friend, hurting people are doubting the life of Christ in us, you and me: "Unless I see your wounds, I will not believe it. Unless I see your scars, I cannot trust your message of hope and resurrection."

By nature, I am a private person. I love to discuss thoughts and ideas, but I have a hard time sharing feelings and experiences. Some years ago, God showed me that this flesh-pattern in me needed to go to the cross. I had to face the fact that it was my flesh that disliked the feeling of being exposed and vulnerable. "Jennifer," He seemed to say to me, "I am not asking you to tell your story. I am asking you to tell My story in its 'Jennifer edition.' You are not your own." I must admit to you that still when God calls on me to share something that is intensely personal to me, it is excruciating. It is still a crucifixion. Even this is hard for me to write. But never has God required me to submit to this crucifixion that I did not experience resurrection. God's work in my life has overflowed in comfort and encouragement and power to someone else. "Therefore I will boast all the more gladly about my weaknesses, so that Christ's power may rest on me" (2 Cor. 12:9).

At the places where I am broken, the power of Christ is authenticated in me for others. Where I have submitted to the crucifixion, the power of the resurrection is put on display. I can say, "Look at my wounds. Touch my scars. I have death-wounds, but I am alive." I can wear my wounds without shame. They tell a resurrection story.

• What are your death-wounds?

_____

_____

_____

• Describe an experience in which you received the supernatural comfort of the Father. Did that comfort, in any measure, come through someone else?

_____

_____

_____

• Has God put anyone in your path who needs the very comfort you have received? What is God telling you to do?

_____

_____

_____

Celebration

Celebrate and worship. Looking to the Spirit for guidance, take time to give careful thought to the enormity of the Father's love for you. Think about His love concretely and tangibly. Celebrate His love.

~ Day 39 ~

Centering

Begin with centering prayer. In the inner sanctuary of your soul, stand before the Father with your arms outstretched and your hands lifted to Him. Ask Him to fill your soul with His abundance. Open your life to His power and provision. Don't rush—speak to Him about your openness and listen for His word to you.

Meditation

We have this treasure in jars of clay to show that this all-surpassing power is from God and not from us. (2 Cor. 4:7)

You and I are clay jars into which the Father has poured His presence, His power, His Spirit. What is the requirement for a clay jar? What does the Father need from you to fill you with Himself? He needs your emptiness.

> The wife of a man from the company of the prophets cried out to Elisha, "Your servant my husband is dead, and you know that he revered the LORD. But now his creditor is coming to take my two boys as his slaves."
>
> Elisha replied to her, "How can I help you? Tell me, what do you have in your house?"
>
> "Your servant has nothing there at all," she said, "except a little oil."
>
> Elisha said, "Go around and ask all your neighbors for empty jars. Don't ask for just a few. Then go inside and shut the door behind you and your sons. Pour oil into all the jars, and as each is filled, put it to one side."

She left him and afterward shut the door behind her and her sons. They brought the jars to her and she kept pouring. When all the jars were full, she said to her son, "Bring me another one." But he replied, "There is not a jar left." *Then the oil stopped flowing.* (2 Kings 4:1–6, italics added)

As you allow the Spirit to translate the Father's message to you from this passage, keep in mind that in Scripture any reference to clay jars or clay in any form represents human beings. Any reference to oil depicts the Holy Spirit.

Have you recognized your own emptiness? Have you realized this: "For I know that nothing good dwells in me, that is, in my flesh; for the wishing is present in me, but the doing of the good is not" (Rom. 7:18, NASB). Have you become convinced that your flesh cannot produce anything that is of eternal value? Have you conceded that you must turn away from yourself and cry out to the Father, throwing yourself at His mercy, to find the fullness you so desperately need?

When you look at this story from the life of Elisha, what did the woman have? She had "a little oil." Because of this, I think this story is directed to believers—people who have the Holy Spirit in them. If you have accepted Jesus Christ as your personal Savior, then you have all of the Holy Spirit in you. But you may not have the fullness of the Spirit.

In order to increase the measure of the oil she already possessed, what did Elisha instruct the woman to do? He told her to bring all the emptiness she could find. Emptiness became valuable because it was the way to fullness. Emptiness was an asset because it provided the necessary condition for abundance. Have you learned to embrace your emptiness when the Father shows it to you? Or are you still trying to cover over and disguise your emptiness? Are you trying to fill your emptiness with things that are not eternal? Are you attempting to find some fullness in the resources of your flesh?

Notice how this story ends. When there was no emptiness left to be filled, the oil stopped flowing. How can we keep our lives open to the continual outpouring of the Spirit? By pouring out to others what He has poured into us.

As your emptiness is filled with His fullness, you have a never-ending supply of oil to dispense to those around you. When ministry is in the flesh, it will drain you dry. When it is in the Spirit, it will open you to a further, deeper infilling of power.

- Bring your emptiness to Him. Let the Spirit speak to you about the empty places in you. Welcome His word to you. Write down what He shows you.

_____

_____

_____

- What are the places that were once empty, but now are filled to overflowing with the life of Christ? Write down what He shows you.

_____

_____

_____

- What is the fullness that you need to be pouring out to others? Let Him speak to you. Write down what He says.

_____

_____

_____

Celebration

Celebrate and worship. Looking to the Spirit for guidance, take time to give careful thought to the enormity of the Father's love for you. Think about His love concretely and tangibly. Celebrate His love.

~ Day 40 ~

Review and Reflect

- Describe the areas of brokenness that are in your life. Invite the Father to put His power on display at those places.

_____

_____

_____

_____

_____

_____

- What flesh-patterns is God in the process of breaking? What flesh are you currently surrendering to crucifixion?

_____

_____

_____

- What does this verse mean to you?
    That is why, for Christ's sake, I delight in weaknesses,
    in insults, in hardships, in persecutions, in difficulties.
    For when I am weak, then I am strong. (2 Cor. 12:10)

_____

_____

_____

Forty-Day Review

- What changes have occurred in your life and thinking?

\
\
\
\
\
\
\
\

- What one concept has impacted you most and why?

\
\
\
\
\
\
\
\

SECTION 3
AN EXTENDED RETREAT

Create the extended retreat that meets your needs and
speaks to your longings. The important element
of your extended retreat is not what you do,
but that you are taking time away
to focus on God and seek His face.

An Extended Retreat: Introduction

You will find that as you spend forty days focusing on hearing from God, your desire for time with Him will increase. You will look for ways to spend more and more time in undistracted waiting on Him. You may want to plan an extended personal retreat.

An extended personal retreat will rejuvenate you spiritually, emotionally, and physically. It will provide the time frame and the setting in which the Father can work in you and speak to you without distraction. During this set-aside time, you can orient all of your activities and thoughts—both waking and sleeping—around Him.

An extended retreat may be a few hours, or it may be twenty-four hours. Whatever time block is realistic for you, plan for an extended time of solitude and silence. Ideally you would plan to be away from your home or work environment simply because you could escape the sense of responsibility and the pull of the work that always needs to be done. You could be beyond the reach of telephones and daily interruptions. However, if it is not possible for you to get away, you can plan for uninterrupted solitude wherever you are.

The following pages are a suggested plan for an extended retreat. You may be doing this retreat alone or with others. If you are retreating as a group, I suggest that you plan much time alone with periodic times of sharing what God is saying.

This plan is only a suggestion. Create the extended retreat that meets your needs and speaks to your longings. The important element of your extended retreat is not what you do, but that you are taking time away to focus on God and seek His face.

This retreat plan includes a series of meditations built around the pattern of tabernacle worship. The tabernacle was a copy and shadow of eternal reality (Heb. 8:5). Each stage of tabernacle worship is a two-layered picture. Each stage shows Jesus Christ, adding depth to our understanding of Him and His redemptive work. Each stage also represents a feature of the human make-up, showing us how to surrender more fully to Him.

The tabernacle pictures both sides of the salvation relationship: Christ is in me and I am in Christ. If you would like to do further reading on the tabernacle, I have listed some resources in section 4.

As you work through the meditations, do so with the expectation that God will speak to you. Be listening for Him. Complete a meditation, then go do something else—walk, relax, or listen to music. Don't rush through them.

Finally, please do not feel guilty if you nap periodically during your extended retreat. This is to be a restorative time for you. As you fill your time with meditating on God's Word and allowing Him to think His thoughts in you, even when you're sleeping, your subconscious mind is still communing with the Father. In fact, specifically ask Him to continue speaking to you while you sleep. He will restore your soul.

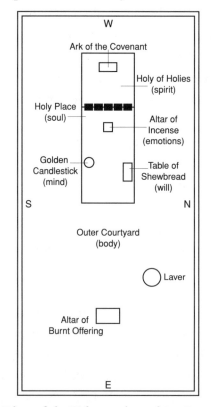

Plan of the Tabernacle and its Courts

An Extended Retreat: Meditations

Meditation 1

Open your heart to the presence of God. Spend these moments preparing your heart to receive *all* of His love. Pray this prayer slowly and reflectively, allowing each thought to take deep root in your heart.

> Father, I want all of You. There is nothing in me that I want to hold on to more than I want to be filled with You. I release all that I am to all that You are.

Open your life to His purposes.

> "For I know the plans I have for you," declares the LORD, "plans to prosper you and not to harm you, plans to give you hope and a future." (Jer. 29:11)
>
> The LORD will fulfill his purpose for me. (Ps. 138:8)

Respond to Him: _____

_____

_____

_____

_____

_____

_____

_____

Open your life to His ways.

> Show me your ways, O Lord,
>> teach me your paths;
> guide me in your truth and teach me,
>> for you are God my Savior,
>> and my hope is in you all day long. . . .
> All the ways of the Lord are loving and faithful
>> for those who keep the demands of his covenant.
>> (Ps. 25:4–5, 10)

> The Lord is righteous in all his ways
>> and loving toward all he has made. (Ps. 145:17)

Respond to Him:

_____

_____

_____

_____

_____

_____

_____

Open your life to His authority.

> O Lord, you are our Father.
>> We are the clay, you are the potter;
>> we are all the work of your hand. (Isa. 64:8)

Know that the LORD is God.
>   It is he who made us, and we are his;
>   we are his people, the sheep of his pasture. (Ps. 100:3)

Respond to Him:

_____

_____

_____

_____

_____

_____

_____

Open yourself fully to Him.
Experience the love that draws you ever deeper into His heart. Pray this prayer:

>   Your holy Fire now burns within
>   And purges every secret sin.
>   My life, the bush; Your life, the Flame
>   That leaves me nevermore the same.
>
>   A heart like Yours, my one desire.
>   Do Your work, Refiner's Fire.

Meditation 2

Use the eternal pattern for opening your life to God's presence—the pattern He gave when He first instructed Moses to build the tabernacle. The tabernacle pattern of worship teaches that God has opened the place of His presence to us. But it has another message as well. The stages of tabernacle worship teach us how to open our lives to Him to allow Him full access to our minds, our wills, and our emotions.

We don't need more access to Him—Jesus has provided all the access we need—but He needs access to us. He invites us to make ourselves available for His mighty work, first *in us,* then *through us.* We can have all of Him that we make room for. How much of Him do you want?

Respond to Him:

_____

_____

_____

_____

_____

_____

_____

_____

You can enter the courtyard of the tabernacle by only one entryway. Open your life to all that God has prepared for you through the One who is the way, Jesus Christ. Every step you take into the courtyard, celebrate Him. Keep in mind that He makes it possible for you to open your life and receive all that God has made available for you.

As you close this meditation time, spend time worshiping Jesus Christ. Sing songs that exalt Him. Tell Him you love Him. Honor Him with your praise and worship.

Meditation 3

As you enter the courtyard, you first encounter the altar of sacrifice. In your mind's eye, it takes the shape of the cross of Jesus. At the cross, you see that Jesus paid the full price for every sin you have ever committed or will ever commit. He took the full weight of God's wrath against your sin on Himself. He became the sacrifice on the altar in your place.

It may have been a very long time since you thanked Him for the cross. Ask the Spirit to show it to you as if you were seeing it for the first time. Use the words of this wonderful hymn, thinking through them, saying them with all your heart, to worship Him.

> When I survey the wondrous cross,
> On which the Prince of glory died,
> My richest gain I count but loss,
> And pour contempt on all my pride.
>
> Forbid it, Lord, that I should boast,
> Save in the death of Christ, my God;
> All the vain things that charm me most,
> I sacrifice them to His blood.
>
> See, from His head, His hands, His feet,
> Sorrow and love flow mingled down;
> Did e'er such love and sorrow meet,
> Or thorns compose so rich a crown?
>
> Were the whole realm of nature mine,
> That were a present far too small;
> Love so amazing, so divine,
> Demands my soul, my life, my all.[20]

Now the cross becomes your altar. The altar on which He calls you to place yourself as a living sacrifice.

I urge you, brothers, in view of God's mercy, to offer your bodies as living sacrifices, holy and pleasing to God—this is your
spiritual act of worship. (Rom. 12:1)

Close your eyes and, with the eyes of your heart, see yourself at the altar—
the empty cross. Prepare your heart. Ask the Spirit to speak clearly to you,
to surface the things that He wants to speak to you about. Tell Him that you
have no other desire except to respond honestly and openly to His voice. As
you place each part of you that the Spirit brings to mind on the altar, name
it. Tell Him, "This is Yours. Use it however You want. You own this now."

On the altar, place all that you are, all that you have been, and all that
you will be.

Respond to Him: _____

_____

_____

_____

_____

Place on the altar your past—every hurt, every mistake, every good memory, every painful memory.

Respond to Him: _____

_____

_____

_____

_____

Place on the altar your present—your joys, your struggles, your needs, your ongoing hurts; those things that bring you pleasure and those things that bring you pain. Surrender each one with these words: "This is Yours, Lord. Create from it what You will."

Respond to Him: _____

_____

_____

_____

_____

Place there your relationships. Let the Spirit walk you through each important relationship in your life and let Him speak to You about each one. Turn them over, one by one. Pause long enough to listen.

Respond to Him: _____

_____

_____

_____

_____

Place on the altar your desires and dreams. Name them. Surrender them. Trust Him with them. The desires He has for you are not less satisfying than the desires you have for yourself. His plans for you are beyond your imagination.

Most likely your own desires are a watered-down or scaled-back version of His desires. Release them to Him so He can do more than you can ask or imagine. Make this your prayer: "What You will. As You will. When You will."

Respond to Him:

_____

_____

_____

_____

_____

Offer Him your body through which He may act out His righteousness. Offer the parts of your body as living sacrifices, no longer instruments of unrighteousness, but now instruments of righteousness. Ask Him to speak through your mouth. Ask Him to work and to touch with your hands. Ask Him to use your feet to go where He wants to go in your world.

Survey all that you have placed on the altar. See the fire from heaven come down to consume it. His presence changes it all into something entirely different, because the altar, consecrated by the blood of the Lamb, is holy, and everything that touches it becomes holy (Exod. 29:37). *Holy* means set aside exclusively for the Lord's use.

Meditation 4

Move through the courtyard to encounter the bronze laver or basin, the place of cleansing. This was a receptacle filled with water where the priest washed his hands and feet before entering the Holy Place.

You have already been cleansed internally at the altar of sacrifice. An ongoing cleansing is always in process as the life of Jesus flows through you, washing away toxins as blood does, bringing new, fresh life to your soul. But you have to be continually washed of the world that clings to you.

An interesting fact about the laver is that it is made out of bronze mirrors. When you look into the laver, you see truth reflected, the truth about yourself. James 1:23–24 says that the person who looks into the Word of God and doesn't change in response to it is like a person who has looked into the mirror, then walked away and forgotten what he saw. So the basin represents the Word of God, and specifically, the place where sin is brought to your attention.

But the water in the laver also represents the word Jesus spoke. Jesus said that you are washed clean by the word He spoke (John 15:3). At the same place where you are confronted with your sin, you are given sin's detergent. Where sin abounds, grace abounds all the more.

Let the Spirit speak to you about elements of the world that are clinging to you—residue He wants to wash away. Is there a situation in your life that causes you to confront your flesh-life? Maybe you've been pleading with God to take it away, but He's answering, "No, I need this situation to reveal your self-life. I'm not going to take away the situation. I'm going to take away your fleshly reaction to the situation." Will you let Him do as He pleases? Listen to Him.

Respond to Him: _____

_____

_____

_____

_____

Meditation 5

Walk deeper into the life of the Spirit. Go inside the tabernacle, leaving the outer court and entering the Holy Place. Open your life further to His indwelling presence, becoming more available for His filling.

The beauty of the tabernacle is hidden to those outside. From outside, there is no form or comeliness that causes one to desire it. The splendor is only experienced from inside. Only within the context of a personal, genuine relationship with Jesus as Lord and Savior can His true beauty be seen. As you surrender all of your being to Him and let Him bring holiness to your life, He manifests His beautiful presence.

Respond to Him:

Meditation 6

Inside the tabernacle, move to the first piece of furniture, the lampstand. You are drawn to it because it is the only source of light in the tabernacle. No windows exist to allow light from the outside. The only illumination is the light of this menorah, a sevenfold lampstand.

Jesus indwelling you with His very life is the illumination that causes you to be able to see and understand the truths of the spiritual realm. It is His life operating in you that brings faith into being because faith requires that you see what is invisible to the physical eye. Faith requires that the eyes of your heart be enlightened so that "you may know the hope to which he has called you, the riches of his glorious inheritance in the saints, and his incomparably great power for us who believe" (Eph. 1:18–19).

The lampstand is the picture of your mind—your intellect and reasoning ability—illuminated by the life of Jesus. Here, surrender this element of your soul. Ask Him to sanctify your mind: your imagination, your intelligence, your thought patterns, your memories.

In His presence, facing His light, ask Him for deeper insight into the things of the Spirit. Ask Him to enlighten the eyes of your heart. Invite Him to bring the light of His presence into every corner of your mind.

Respond to Him:

_____

_____

_____

_____

_____

Meditation 7

The lampstand is fueled by olive oil. In Scripture, oil is always the picture of the Holy Spirit. The Spirit of Christ is the fuel that energizes your life when you operate from your spirit-core. Just as the lampstand had to be continually filled with oil, you are to be continually filled with the Spirit. Just as the lamp was never to go out, so your life is to burn without interruption. The Word gives two commands along these lines:

- Be continually filled and refilled with the Spirit (Eph. 5:18).
- Don't quench the Spirit (1 Thess. 5:19).

Spend time asking the Father to fill you with His spirit. Ask Him to fill you to overflowing. Ask Him to fill you so full that He flushes out anything that is cluttering your heart.

Respond to Him:

_____

_____

_____

_____

Imagine a priest being anointed with the anointing oil as the Lord commanded. The oil was poured over his head. It dripped off his hair and off his beard and ran down over his vestments and onto the ground. Ask Jesus to pour out His Spirit on your life to such a degree that your life drips with the power of the Spirit.

Wait in His presence. Give Him time.

Respond to Him: _____

_____

_____

_____

_____

Now, let Jesus Himself be the flame that ignites the oil. Ask Him to show you anything in your life that is causing the fire to go out. Offer up anything that is quenching the Spirit.

Respond to Him: _____

_____

_____

_____

_____

Meditation 8

Still in the holy place, move to the table of shewbread, or the bread of the Presence. This reminds you that He is not a God far away, but He has put His life into you. Just as your body receives life and nutrients from food, your soul receives life from Him. Just as your body becomes a partaker of the food you eat because your cells absorb its life, so your soul becomes a partaker of His nature as your life absorbs His life and He begins to express Himself through you.

> Grace and peace be multiplied to you in the knowledge of God and of Jesus our Lord; seeing that His divine power has granted to us everything pertaining to life and godliness, through the true knowledge of Him who called us by His own glory and excellence. For by these He has granted to us His precious and magnificent promises, in order that by them you might become partakers of the divine nature, having escaped the corruption that is in the world by lust. (2 Pet. 1:2–4, NASB)

Respond to Him: _____

_____

_____

_____

_____

_____

The bread of the Presence represents your will. As you are fully indwelt by His life, He begins to transform your desires and your will. "For it is God who works in you to will . . . according to his good purpose" (Phil. 2:13). Jesus is expressing His will and His desires through you. What is His will? "'My food,' said Jesus, 'is to do the will of him who sent me and to finish his work'" (John 4:34). As you feast on the bread of the Presence, realize that your food is to do the will of Him who sent you.

Surrender this aspect of your soul. Tell Him that you release every desire other than the desire to do His will.

Respond to Him:

_____

_____

_____

_____

Meditation 9

Move to the altar of incense, the place of intercession. On this altar, incense burns over ashes taken from the altar of sacrifice. Our privilege of interceding has its basis in the blood of Jesus. Jesus fulfilled the required payment for your sin-debt and made you a priest, with the awesome privilege and responsibility to intercede.

At the altar of incense, having yielded both your mind and your will to Him, allow Him to fill your emotions. Let Him pour His love into your heart as you let it rise to Him in intercession (Rom. 5:5). As He has filled your mind with His thoughts; as He has filled your will with His desires; now He will fill your emotions with His emotions. As you yield yourself to His presence, you will feel the Spirit of the Son in you crying out, "'*Abba,* Father'" (Rom. 8:15; Gal. 4:6).

Take time in His presence, still before Him, worshiping at His feet. Allow Him to fill you with His love and His desires for those for whom you would intercede. Don't rush in and intercede out of your earth-bound, time-bound love. Let His love rise up in you.

Respond to Him:

_____

_____

_____

_____

Meditation 10

Now stand before the veil which conceals the Holy of Holies, the very presence of the living God, and Jesus, robed in majesty, honored, and exalted. Before you walk through the veil to pour yourself out in pure worship, with your life fully open to Him, again thank Him that He initiated the way and opened the veil so that you can live in His presence.

Take time to be filled with reverence. Take time to consider what an astounding privilege it is. Take time to consider what it cost the Son and what it cost the Father to open a new and living way into the Holy of Holies.

Respond to Him: _____

_____

_____

_____

_____

_____

Meditation 11

Come before His throne with thanksgiving and praise. Encounter the living God with pure worship and adoration. In your inner sanctuary, take a position of worship before Him and worship with abandon. Lose yourself in Him. Let everything else fade away and focus your heart on Him. Here, your body and soul now fully surrendered to Him, worship Him in spirit and in truth.

> Father, as I soak myself in Your presence, saturate me with Yourself. Seep into my spirit pores until I am filled with You. Let me breathe in Your love for me and breathe it out again toward You. You are my treasure and my heart knows no other home.[21]

Respond to Him:

_____

_____

_____

_____

_____

Meditation 12

Does there seem to be a central theme in all that God is saying to you right now? What is the essence of the thought He is pressing on you?

Respond to Him:

_____

_____

_____

_____

_____

SECTION 4
RESOURCES

For Further Study

Books by Jennifer Kennedy Dean:

Live a Praying Life: Open Your Life to God's Power and Provision
This resource compiles all of Jennifer Kennedy Dean's works on prayer into a comprehensive thirteen-week study. New material is included. Study groups, prayer groups, and individuals will all gain insight through interactive questions and prayer-journaling exercises. The complexities of prayer are handled through an open, intelligent, and meaningful look at Scripture.

Riches Stored in Secret Places: A Devotional Guide for Those Who Hunger after the Deep Things of God
In this exciting twelve-week devotional guide, Dean shows readers how to uncover the layers of truth hidden in Scripture. Readers who long to hear God speak from His Word will find clear direction and encouragement as Dean teaches her methods for contemplative prayer, guided by God's Word. Each week readers will delve into a passage of Scripture and will practice daily journaling, prayer, and listening exercises that will catapult them along a lifetime course of hearing God. The components of this book are flexible for use in small groups, prayer partnerships, or in one-on-one mentoring relationships. Author Marilynn Carlson Webber calls *Riches Stored in Secret Places* "a modern devotional classic for today's Christian."

Secret Place of the Most High: A Journal for Those Who Hunger after the Deep Things of God
Journaling has long been a discipline practiced by those seeking deeper intimacy with God. In this resource, Dean provides topics, meditations, and prayers to explore and expound upon in journaling exercises. Beautifully designed and beautifully written, this tool will be valuable to the beginner as well as the experienced journaler. Fresh, reverent, and inspiring, *Secret Place of the Most High* calls believers to new levels of intimacy with the Father.

Power Praying: Prayer that Produces Results

With the release of this third volume in a trilogy on prayer, Jennifer Kennedy Dean proves once again that the truth about prayer's power lies beyond scripted, pat slogans. Dean continues to help us expand our limiting definitions of prayer and understand that prayer has no set formulas. In this book, Dean explains the key to praying with consistent power: living moment-by-moment in the Spirit's present-tense life. She cuts through the frills to the heart of truth as she communicates the living Jesus, the power of God working through His blood, what it means to have spiritual vision and a living, active faith, and God's purpose and method for purifying His "power pray-ers."

The Praying Life: Living Beyond Your Limits

"With so many books about prayer, can anything new or fresh be said? 'Probably not,' I thought as I began to read *The Praying Life*. I was happy to find this book refreshing and challenging" *(Bookstore Journal)*. The consensus on this book affirms it is unusually insightful, straightforward, and deep. In it, Dean addresses some universal questions about prayer: If God is sovereign, why do we pray? Does prayer have an impact on the earth, or is it just a reflective activity? Is prayer more than a conversation between two parties? Dean's imaginative and original use of illustrations to teach deep truth is well-known, and this book proves she deserves that acclaim. She avoids time-worn cliches, yet she presents the truth without compromise.

Heart's Cry: Principles of Prayer

This extraordinary book contains twelve sections, each dealing with a scriptural principle of prayer. Each section ends with a meditation, reflection questions, and review questions. You will find *Heart's Cry* the perfect tool for personal devotionals, small group studies on prayer, or one-on-one mentoring relationships. This little book is so rich and so packed with wisdom and clear biblical teaching, it has already been called "a classic." Cynthia Heald, author of *Becoming A Woman of Prayer* (NavPress), quotes it in the company of the classic thinkers and devotional writers. This is a "must" for your prayer library.

Books that address dying to the flesh

MotherWise: Freedom for Mothers by Denise Glenn (Sisters, Ore.: Multnomah, 1999).

Lifetime Guarantee by Bill Gillham (Brentwood, Tenn.: Wolgemuth & Hyatt, 1987).

Handbook to Happiness by Charles R. Solomon (Wheaton, Ill.: Tyndale House, 1971).

The Saving Life of Christ by Major Ian Thomas (Grand Rapids, Mich.: Zondervan, 1961).

The Release of the Spirit by Watchman Nee (Indianapolis, Ind.: Sure Foundation, 1965).

Books that address the tabernacle worship

A Woman's Heart: God's Dwelling Place. An In-depth Study of the Old Testament Tabernacle by Beth Moore (Nashville, Tenn.: LifeWay Press, 1995).

All for His Glory by Aletha Hinthorn (Kansas City, Mo.: Beacon Hill Press, 1998).

The Tabernacle by M. R. DeHaan (Grand Rapids, Mich.: Lamplighter Books, Zondervan, 1955).

The Tabernacle of Israel: Its Structure and Symbolism by James Strong (Grand Rapids, Mich.: Kregel Publications, 1987).

The Tabernacle, the Priesthood, and the Offerings by Henry W. Soltau (Grand Rapids, Mich.: Kregel Publications, 1998).

Endnotes

1. Andrew Murray, *The Holiest of All* (Old Tappan, N.J.: Fleming H. Revell Co.), 86.

2. Donald Coggan, *Preaching: The Sacrament of the Word* (New York: The Crossroad Publishing Co., 1987), 168.

3. Anne Morrow Lindbergh, *Gift from the Sea* (New York: Pantheon Books, 1955, 1975), 10–11.

4. Jennifer Kennedy Dean, *Heart's Cry* (Birmingham, Ala.: New Hope, 1992), 198.

5. John Woolman, *The Journal of John Woolman,* 8, 10–11.

6. Helen H. Lemmel, "Turn Your Eyes Upon Jesus."

7. Thomas R. Kelley, *A Testament of Devotion* (New York: Harper & Row, 1941), 29.

8. William Law, *A Serious Call to a Devout and Holy Life* (Grand Rapids, Mich.: Wm. B. Eerdmans, 1966), 143.

9. E. M. Bounds, *Power through Prayer,* quoted in *The Best of E. M. Bounds on Prayer* (Grand Rapids, Mich.: Baker Book House, 1981), 95.

10. Evan Drake Howard, *Centered in God* (Minneapolis, Minn.: Augsburg Fortress, 1995), xiv.

11. Kelley, *A Testament of Devotion,* 44.

12. C. S. Lewis, *Letters to Malcolm* (Glasgow, Scotland: Fount Paperbacks, 1978), 70.

13. Kelley, *A Testament of Devotion,* 45.

14. Major Ian Thomas, *The Saving Life of Christ* (Grand Rapids, Mich.: Zondervan, 1961), 41.

15. Richard J. Foster, *Finding the Heart's True Home* (San Francisco: HarperSan Francisco, 1992), 54.

16. Dean, *Heart's Cry,* 11–12, 15.

17. Jennifer Kennedy Dean, *Power Praying,* (Blue Springs, Mo.: Master's Touch, 1997), 61–72.

18. Jennifer Kennedy Dean, *Secret Place of the Most High* (Birmingham, Ala.: New Hope, 1996), 112.
19. C. S. Lewis, *Reflections on the Psalms* (Orlando, Fla.: Harcourt Brace & Company, 1958, 1986), 94–95.
20. Isaac Watts, "When I Survey the Wondrous Cross."
21. Dean, *Secret Place of the Most High,* 12.

About the Author

Jennifer Kennedy Dean
The Praying Life Foundation
P.O. Box 62
Blue Springs, MO 64013
(888) 844-6647 or (816) 228-8899
Fax: (816) 228-0925
E-mail: jenniferkdean@prayinglife.org
Internet: www.prayinglife.org